Keto Dessert Cookbook 2020

quick & easy, sugar-free, ketogenic cakes & sweets, smoothies to shed weight

By: Debbie J. Jenkins

© Copyright 2020 by Debbie J. Jenkins - All rights reserved.

This document is geared towards providing exact and reliable information in regards to the topic and issue covered. The publication is sold with the idea that the publisher is not required to render accounting, officially permitted, or otherwise, qualified services. If advice is necessary, legal or professional, a practiced individual in the profession should be ordered.

- From a Declaration of Principles which was accepted and approved equally by a Committee of the American Bar Association and a Committee of Publishers and Associations.

In no way is it legal to reproduce, duplicate, or transmit any part of this document in either electronic means or in printed format. Recording of this publication is strictly prohibited and any storage of this document is not allowed unless with written permission from the publisher. All rights reserved.

The information provided herein is stated to be truthful and consistent, in that any liability, in terms of inattention or otherwise, by any usage or abuse of any policies, processes, or directions contained within is the solitary and utter responsibility of the recipient reader. Under no circumstances will any legal responsibility or blame be held against the publisher for any reparation, damages, or monetary loss due to the information herein, either directly or indirectly.

Respective authors own all copyrights not held by the publisher.

The information herein is offered for informational purposes solely, and is universal as so. The presentation of the information is without contract or any type of guarantee assurance.

The trademarks that are used are without any consent, and the publication of the trademark is without permission or backing by the trademark owner.

Table of Contents

Introduction
Chapter 1: Benefits and Foods You Can and Cannot Eat Using Keto
Chapter 2: Muffins & Bagels
- Almond & Apple Maple Muffins
- Banana Avocado Muffins
- Blueberry Flaxseed Muffins
- Cinnamon Walnut Flax Muffins
- Coconut Lemon Muffins
- Peanut Butter Muffins - Instant Pot
- Pecan Pie & Chocolate Muffins
- Pumpkin & Maple Flaxseed Muffins

Bagels
- Cinnamon Raisin Bagels

Chapter 3: Cakes
Regular Cakes
- Carrot & Almond Cake
- Chocolate & Zucchini Cake
- Chocolate Lava Cake
- Glazed Pound Cake
- Gooey Butter Cake
- Orange Rum Cake
- Pumpkin Bread
- Slow-Cooked Raspberry Coconut Cake

Bar Cakes
- Almond Coconut Bars
- Cheesecake Mocha Bars
- Chocolate Peppermint Cookie Bars
- Coconut Bars
- Keto Magic Bars
- Mixed Berry Cake Bars
- Peanut Butter Protein Bars

Cupcakes & Mug Cakes

- Blueberry Cupcakes
- Brownie Mug Cake - Instant Pot
- Chocolate Mug Cake
- Pumpkin Spice Cupcakes
- Sour Cream Vanilla Cupcakes
- Vanilla Berry Mug Cake
- Zucchini Spiced Cupcakes

Chapter 4: Fat Bombs & Pies

- Blackberry Coconut Fat Bombs
- Blueberry Fat Bombs
- Cheesecake Surprise Fat Bombs
- Chocolate Chip Cookie Dough Fat Bomb
- Cocoa Butter Walnut Fat Bombs
- Coconut Macaroon Fat Bombs
- Coconut Orange Creamsicle Fat Bombs
- Coffee Fat Bombs
- Dark Chocolate Fat Bombs
- Lemon Cheesecake Fat Bombs
- Neapolitan Fat Bombs
- Orange & Walnut Chocolate Fat Bombs
- Peppermint & Chocolate Fat Bombs
- Stuffed Pecan Fat Bombs

Pies

- Creamy Lime Pie
- Pumpkin Cheesecake Pie
- Sour Cream Lemon Pie
- Low-Carb Almond Flour Crust
- Mini Coconut Pies

Chapter 5: Delicious Mousse & Pudding Options

- Cheesecake Pudding
- Chocolate & Avocado Pudding
- Cinnamon Roll Mousse In A Jar
- Peanut Butter Mousse
- Pumpkin Custard
- Raspberry Chia Pudding

White Chocolate Mousse

Chapter 6: Frozen Desserts

Butter Pecan Ice Cream
Coconut Ice Cream
Egg-Fast Vanilla Frozen Custard
Peanut Butter Ice Cream
Pistachio Ice Cream
Thick Dark Chocolate Milkshake

Smoothies

Almond & Blueberry Smoothie
Avocado Smoothie
Avocado Mint Green Smoothie
Banana Bread - Blueberry Smoothie
Blackberry Cheesecake Smoothie
Blueberry Yogurt Smoothie
Chocolate & Cinnamon Smoothie
Cinnamon Roll Smoothie
Cucumber Spinach Smoothies
Delightful Chocolate Smoothie
Mexican Chocolate Smoothie
Mint Chocolate Smoothie
Mocha Smoothie
Pecan Pie Smoothie
Smoothie In A Bowl
Strawberry & Rhubarb Pie Smoothie
Strawberry Smoothies
Vanilla Fat-Burning Smoothie

Chapter 7: Snacks

Apple Cider Donut Bites
Baked Almonds & Brie
Baked Apples
Blueberry Tart
Chocolate Coconut Bites
Cinnamon Vanilla Protein Bites
Cream Cheese Truffles

    Peanut Butter & Coconut Balls
    Pumpkin Blondies
    Strawberries With Coconut Whip
    Strawberry & Cream Cakes
    Strawberry Rhubarb Crumble
    White Chocolate Bark
  Cookies
    Chocolate-Filled Peanut Butter Cookies
    Chocolate Fudge Haystacks
    Chocolate Sea Salt Cookies
    Coconut Chocolate Cookies
    Italian Almond Macaroons
    Pecan Turtle Truffles
    Pumpkin Cheesecake Cookies
    Strawberry Thumbprint Delights
    Streusel Scones
    Walnut Cookies

Conclusion
Index For The Recipes
Description

Introduction

Congratulations on purchasing *Ketogenic Sweet Treats Cookbook* and thank you for doing so. Your new cookbook will provide you with many new ways to change your lifestyle. You will never be hungry and will still remain within the constraints of the keto plan while fulfilling your 'sweet tooth' as you choose.

I am delighted that you have chosen to take a new path using the keto diet plan to help you prepare delicious, yet healthy desserts without going out of the state of ketosis. The plan goes by many different names such as the low-carb diet, keto diet, and the low-carbohydrate diet & high-fat (LCHF) diet plan.

The following chapters will discuss the benefits of the keto diet as well as what foods you can enjoy and the ones that should be avoided. Each of the recipes includes the number of servings as well as the macros including the protein, net carbs, fat content, and calories. The foods are grouped according to their category from muffins to ice cream, you will always have a sweet option available.

Let's get started!

Chapter 1: Benefits and Foods You Can and Cannot Eat Using Keto

As you begin your ketogenic journey, you will have many questions. This segment will enlighten you so you can begin using a few simple questions.

What are the benefits of the ketogenic diet?

The high-fat combined with the low-carb foods is a hit in this fabulous collection of desserts. The low-carbohydrate diet plan has many benefits including:

- Its initial use for epilepsy
- Increased vitality and energy
- Accelerated fat loss
- Lowered blood sugar
- Lowered cholesterol
- Improved mental clarity or focus

What can you eat with the ketogenic diet?

Whole Eggs: Visit your local area market for free-range options. You can scramble, fry, boil, or devil eggs up for a picnic or any occasion for a quick snack.

Grass-Fed Butter: You can promote fat loss and butter is almost carb-free. The butter is a naturally occurring fatty acid which is rich in conjugated linoleic acid (CLA). It is suitable for maintaining weight loss and retaining lean muscle mass.

Ghee is also a great staple for your keto stock which is also called clarified butter.

Heavy Whipping Cream: This is an option almost unbelievable with only 5 grams of fat per tablespoon.

Also - Include These Cold Items:
- Full-fat sour cream
- Goat cheese
- Full-fat cream cheese
- Parmesan cheese
- Hard & Soft cheeses – ex. mozzarella or sharp cheddar

Dairy-Free Substitutions:
- Unsweetened Almond Milk
- Flax Milk
- Full-Fat Coconut Milk
- Macadamia Milk
- Hemp Milk

Flour Substitutes:
- Almond Flour
- Coconut Flour
- Almond Meal
- Flax Meal
- Sunflower Seed Or Pumpkin Seed Meal
- Ground & Whole Psyllium Husk Powder
- Sesame Flour

Keto Sweeteners:
- *Stevia Drops* offer delicious flavors including hazelnut, vanilla, English toffee, and chocolate. Some individuals think the drops are too bitter, so at first, use only three drops to equal one teaspoon of sugar.

- *Swerve Granular Sweetener* is also an excellent choice as a blend. It's made from non-digestible carbs sourced from starchy root veggies and select fruits. Start with 3/4 of a teaspoon for every one of sugar. Increase the portion to your taste.

- *Swerve Confectioners Powdered Sugar* for your baking needs. Unfortunately, it's more expensive (about twice the price) than other products such as the Pyure.

- *Xylitol* is at the top of the sugary list as an excellent choice to sweeten your teriyaki and barbecue sauce and teriyaki. Its natural-occurring sugar alcohol has a Glycemic index (GI) standing of 13.

- *Pyure Granulated Stevia* is one of the best all-around sweeteners. Pyure Organic All-Purpose Blend with less of a bitter aftertaste versus a stevia-based product. The blend of stevia and erythritol is an excellent alternative to baking, sweetening desserts, and various cooking needs.

- *Monk Fruit Sweetener* is an extract containing zero carbs and calories, making it a great option for a ketogenic diet. The amount you use can vary between different brands based on what other ingredients may be included in the particular recipe used.

Keto Monounsaturated & Saturated Fats:

Include these items (listed by estimated grams):

- Olives – 3 jumbo - 5 large or 10 small – 1 net carb
- Chicken fat/Duck fat/Beef tallow – 1 tbsp. - 0 net carbs
- Unsweetened flaked coconut – 3 tbsp. - 2 net carbs
- Unsalted butter/Ghee – 1 tbsp. - 0 net carbs
- Egg yolks – 1 large – 0.6 net carbs
- Extra-virgin olive oil - 2 tsp. - 0 carbs.
- Organic red palm oil – ex. Nutiva - 1 tbsp. - 0 net carbs
- Avocado oil/Sesame oil/Flaxseed oil – 1 tbsp. - 0 net carbs

Fruits:

This list of fruits are organized according to your carbohydrate limits and are ½ cup servings (100 grams).

- Apples – no skin - boiled – 13.6 total carbs
- Apricots - 7.5 total carbs
- Bananas - 23.4 total carbs
- Fresh Blackberries - 5.4 net carbs
- Fresh Blueberries - 8.2 net carbs
- Fresh Strawberries - 3 net carbs
- Cantaloupe - 6 total carbs
- Raw Cranberries - 4 net carbs
- Gooseberries - 8.8 net carbs
- Kiwi - 14.2 total carbs
- Fresh Boysenberries - 8.8 net carbs
- Oranges - 11.7 total carbs
- Peaches - 11.6 total carbs
- Pears – 19.2 total carbs
- Pineapple - 11 total carbs
- Plums – 16.3 total carbs
- Watermelon - 7.1 total carbs

Which kind of food should you eat in small quantities?

Grains to Avoid:

First, you need to realize grains are made from carbohydrates. This list is based on one cup servings. Avoid bread, pasta, pizza crusts, or crackers and cookies made with these grains:

- Buckwheat: 33 carbs - 6 protein - 1 grams fat
- Wheat: (1 slice wheat bread) 14 carbs - 3 protein - 1 gram fat
- Barley: 44 carbs - 4 protein - 1 gram fat
- Quinoa: 39 carbs - 8 protein - 4 grams fat
- Corn: 32 carbs - 4 protein - 1 grams fat
- Millet: 41 carbs - 6 protein - 2 grams fat
- Bulgur: 33 carbs - 5.6 protein - 0.4 grams fat

- Amaranth: 46 carbs - 9 protein - 4 grams fat
- Oats: 36 carbs - 6 protein - 3 grams fat
- Rice: 45 carbs - 5 protein - 2 grams fat
- Rye: 15 carbs - 3 protein - 1 gram fat

What can't you eat with the ketogenic diet?

Processed Foods:

Don't purchase any items if you see carrageenan on the label. Generally, look for labels with the least amount of ingredients. Usually, the ones that provide the most nutrition are listed in those shorter lists. These are just a few examples of processed snacks to avoid while on a ketogenic diet.

- Cereal Bars
- Rice cakes
- Popcorn
- Flavored Nuts
- Potato Chips
- Crackers/Pretzels
- Protein Bars

Processed Meats: While protein is an undeniably important part of a healthy diet, seeking your protein from meats which have been treated will overload your body full of chemicals. The processed meats tend to be lower in protein while higher in sodium and contain preservatives that can cause a variety of health risks including asthma and heart disease. Choose from the quality cuts of meat found in most grocery stores.

Non-Organic Milk: Despite being touted as part of a balanced diet; non-organic milk is routinely found to be full of growth hormones as well as 'pusses as a result of over-milking. The growth hormones leave behind antibiotics, which in turn, makes it more difficult for the human body to counter infections as well as causing an increased chance of colon cancer, prostate cancer, and breast cancer.

White Flour: Much like processed meats, by the time white flour has completed the processing, it's utterly devoid of any nutritional value. According to *Care2*, white flour, when consumed as part of a regular diet, has been shown to increase a woman's chance of breast cancer by a shocking 200%.

Why should you eat desserts?

It is important for you to enjoy a 'keto-friendly' dessert when the urge strikes. You now have a ton of recipes to prepare and stash for those times when you must have a sweet treat. Just to prove a point, take a look at this delicious

Chocolate Sauce recipe you can drizzle over your favorite cake or ice cream selection:

Yields Provided: 8 servings
Nutritional Macros - One Individual Serving:
- 1.23 g Net Carbs
- 1.8 g Protein
- 14.9 g Total Fats
- 154 Calories

Ingredient List:
- Whipping cream (1 cup)
- Powdered Swerve Sweetener (.33 cup)
- Finely chopped unsweetened chocolate (2.5 oz.)
- Vanilla extract (.5 tsp.)

Preparation Steps:
1. Use the medium heat setting and whisk the whipping cream and sweetener until combined. Once simmering, remove from the heat.
2. Fold in the chocolate. Set aside for five minutes or until the chocolate is completely melted.
3. Whisk in the vanilla extract.
4. Drizzle over your favorite low-carb ice cream or delicious cake.

Enjoy a quick and easy homemade topping, so you can eliminate the risk of choosing an option that may have tons of hidden carbohydrates. Does it look like a diet item to you? It is!

Chapter 2: Muffins & Bagels

Almond & Apple Maple Muffins

Yields Provided: 12 servings
Nutritional Macros - One Individual Serving:
- 10 g Net Carbs
- 5 g Total Protein
- 15 g Total Fats
- 184 Calories

Ingredient List:
- Eggs (2)
- Melted butter (.33 cup)
- Pure maple syrup (4 tbsp.)
- Almond flour (2.5 cups)
- Cinnamon (1 tsp.)
- Thinly sliced apple (1)

Preparation Steps:
1. Heat the oven to reach 350° Fahrenheit.
2. Whisk all of the fixings – omitting the apple.
3. Peel and fold the apple slices. Dump the dough into the cups.
4. Bake for 15 minutes and cool before storing.

Banana Avocado Muffins

Yields Provided: 6 servings
Nutritional Macros - One Individual Serving:
- 4 g Net Carbs
- 30 g Total Fats
- 8 g Total Protein
- 332 Calories

Ingredient List:
- Large eggs (3)
- Monk fruit - 30% extract (.25 tsp.)
- Stevia powder extract (.25 tsp.)
- Vanilla extract (1 tsp.)
- Coconut oil (.25 cup)
- Banana extract (2 tsp.)
- Bak. powder (1 tsp.)
- Coconut flour (.25 cup)
- Cinnamon (.5 tsp.)
- Salt (.25 tsp.)
- Almond flour (.75 cup)
- Mashed avocado (1 medium)
- Pecans (.5 cup chopped)
- *Also Needed*: 6-count muffin tin

Preparation Steps:
1. Leave the eggs out to become room temperature.
2. Warm up the oven to 350° Fahrenheit.
3. Generously grease the muffin tin.
4. Whisk the coconut oil with stevia and monk fruit.
5. Whisk the eggs and mix with the vanilla and banana extracts.
6. In another container, sift or whisk the coconut flour, baking powder, cinnamon, salt, and almond flour.
7. Blend into the coconut oil mixture and the mashed avocado.
8. Fold in the nuts, reserving two tablespoons to sprinkle on top.
9. Empty the batter into the molds and garnish with the nuts.
10. Bake for approximately 25 to 30 minutes.

Blueberry Flaxseed Muffins

Yields Provided: 10 servings
Nutritional Macros - One Individual Serving:
- 8.8 g Net Carbs
- 18.3 g Total Fats
- 7.6 g Total Protein
- 221 Calories

Ingredient List:
- Flaxseeds (1.5 cups)
- Bak. powder (1 tbsp.)
- Eggs (5)
- Vanilla extract (1 tsp.)
- Almond milk (3 tbsp.)
- Coconut oil (4 tbsp.)
- Blueberries (.5 cup)
- Salt (1 pinch)
- Sugar substitute (as desired)

Preparation Steps:
1. Warm up the oven to reach 350° Fahrenheit.
2. Use a coffee grinder to prepare the seeds.
3. Combine each of the dry fixings in a mixing container.
4. Whisk the eggs in a mixing container. Pour in the oil and milk. Stir well.
5. Combine all of the fixings.
6. Fold in the berries and stir gently with a spoon.
7. Pour into muffin cups.
8. Bake for 15 minutes. Cool slightly and serve.

Cinnamon Walnut Flax Muffins

Yields Provided: 12 servings
Nutritional Macros - One Individual Serving:
- 2 g Net Carbs
- 20 g Total Fats
- 6 g Total Protein
- 219 Calories

Ingredient List:
- Ground golden flaxseed or buy flax meal already ground (1 cup)
- Pastured eggs (4)
- Avocado oil or any oil (.5 cup)
- Granulated sweetener - Lakanto coconut sugar, maple sugar erythritol (.5 cup)
- Coconut flour (.25 cup)
- Vanilla extract (2 tsp.)
- Cinnamon (2 tsp.)
- Bak. soda (.5 tsp.)
- Sea salt (1 pinch)
- Lemon juice (1 tsp.)
- *Optional*: Walnuts chopped (1 cup)

Preparation Steps:
1. Warm the oven in advance to 325° Fahrenheit. Prepare the muffin tin with paper liners.
2. If starting with whole golden flaxseed, grind it in a coffee grinder, then measure 1 cup.
3. Mix the fixings in the order they are listed using an electric mixer. Add in walnuts *last* after using a mixer.
4. Bake for 18 to 22 minutes. Serve when ready after slightly cooling.

Coconut Lemon Muffins

Yields Provided: 16 servings
Nutritional Macros - One Individual Serving:
- 2 g Net Carbs
- 7 g Total Fats
- 3 g Total Protein
- 78 Calories

Ingredient List:
- Erythritol (.25 cup)
- Butter (.25 cup)
- Eggs (3)
- Coconut flour (.25 cup)
- Coconut flakes (.5 cup)
- Baking powder (.5 tsp.)
- Vanilla extract (.5 tsp.)
- Coconut milk (3 tbsp.)
- Lemon - juice & zest (1)

Preparation Steps:
1. Warm the oven to 400° Fahrenheit.
2. Lightly grease 16 muffin tins. Whisk the butter and erythritol together until creamy.
3. Break the eggs in one at a time. Add the lemon juice, zest, vanilla extract, and milk. Sift and add the baking powder, flour, and flaked coconut.
4. Scoop the dough into the baking pan.
5. Prepare for 20 minutes in the heated oven. Cool slightly and enjoy. Cool thoroughly before storing.

Peanut Butter Muffins - Instant Pot

Yields Provided: 6 servings
Nutritional Macros - One Individual Serving:
- 5 g Net Carbs
- 14 g Total Fats
- 7 g Total Protein
- 193 Calories

Ingredient List:
- Coconut oil (.5 cup)
- Peanut butter (.5 cup)
- Liquid stevia granulated sweetener (to your liking)
- *Also Needed*: 12-18 count muffin tin & liners or a loaf pan

Preparation Steps:
1. Prepare the tin of choice with a spritz of oil.
2. Combine the oil and peanut butter together on the stovetop or microwave. Melt and add the sweetener.
3. Scoop into the tins or loaf pan and freeze.
4. You can serve with a drizzle of melted chocolate – but remember to count the carbs.

Pecan Pie & Chocolate Muffins

Yields Provided: 12 servings
Nutritional Macros - One Individual Serving:
- 3.4 g Net Carbs
- 4.4 g Total Protein
- 27.1 g Total Fats
- 286 Calories

Ingredient List:
- Swerve Sweetener (.75 cup)
- Pecans - coarsely chopped (1 cup)
- Almond flour (1 cup)
- Salt (1 pinch)
- Softened butter (.5 cup)
- Large eggs (2 unchilled)
- *Optional:* Molasses (1 tbsp.)
- 90% cacao chocolate chopped/sugar-free chocolate chips (2.5 oz.)

Preparation Steps:
1. Warm the oven to reach 325° Fahrenheit.
2. Prepare 12 muffins cups with parchment paper liners or silicone liners work best.
3. Whisk the flour, granulated erythritol, salt, and chopped pecans.
4. Beat the butter, eggs, and molasses together until smooth. Whip in the almond flour mixture until just combined. Stir in the chopped chocolate.
5. Portion into the muffin cups.
6. Bake 26 to 28 minutes, or until set.
7. Let the muffins cool in the pan.

Pumpkin & Maple Flaxseed Muffins

Yields Provided: 10 servings
Nutritional Macros - One Individual Serving:
- 2 g Net Carbs
- 8.5 g Total Fats
- 5 g Total Protein
- 120 Calories

Ingredient List:
- Ground flaxseed (1.25 cups)
- Pumpkin pie spice (1 tbsp.)
- Baking powder (.5 tbsp.)
- Erythritol (.33 cup)
- Salt (.5 tsp.)
- Cinnamon (1 tbsp.)
- Pure pumpkin puree (1 cup)
- Egg (1)
- Maple syrup (.5 tsp.)
- Apple cider vinegar (.5 tsp.)
- Vanilla extract (.5 tsp.)
- Coconut oil (2 tbsp.)
- Garnish: Pumpkin seeds
- *Also Needed:*
- Blender such as NutriBullet
- Muffin tin – 10-count sections with silicone liners

Preparation Steps:
1. Warm the oven to reach 350° Fahrenheit.
2. Prepare the muffin pan with cupcake liners.
3. Add the seeds to the blender about one second – no longer or it could become damp.
4. Combine the dry fixings and whisk until well mixed.
5. Add the vanilla extract, puree, and pumpkin spice along with the maple syrup if using.
6. Blend in the oil, egg, and apple cider vinegar.
7. Combine nuts or any other fold-ins of your choice, but also add the carbs.
8. Scoop the mixture out by the tablespoon into the muffin cups.
9. Garnish with some of the pumpkin seeds. Leave a little space in the top to allow them to rise.
10. Bake until they are slightly browned (20 min.).
11. Let them cool for a few minutes and add some ghee or butter or some more syrup.

Bagels

Cinnamon Raisin Bagels

Yields Provided: 6 servings
Nutritional Macros - One Individual Serving:
- 6 g Net Carbs
- 10 g Total Fats
- 3 g Total Protein
- 139 Calories

Ingredient List:
- Coconut flour sifted (.33 cup)
- Golden flax meal (1.5 tbsp.)
- Baking soda (.5 tsp.)
- *Optional:* Sea salt (a dash)
- Baking powder (1 tsp.)
- Cinnamon (2 tsp.)
- Whisked eggs (3)
- Apple cider vinegar (1 tsp.)
- Unsweetened coconut or almond milk (.33 cup)
- Melted butter - coconut oil or ghee (2.5 tbsp.)
- Liquid stevia (1 tsp.)
- Golden raisins (.33 cup)
- *Optional*: Vanilla extract (1 tsp.)
- *Also Needed:* Donut/bagel pan

Preparation Steps:
1. Warm up the oven to 350° Fahrenheit.
2. Grease the pan.
3. Mix the dry fixings (the golden flax meal, the sifted coconut flour, baking soda, cinnamon, sea salt, and baking powder) thoroughly.
4. In another container, combine the almond/coconut milk, apple cider vinegar, eggs, melted butter/coconut oil, vanilla extract, and stevia.
5. Combine all of the fixings and add to the prepared pan – spreading evenly with a spatula.
6. Bake for 17 to 20 minutes. Cool for three to four minutes.
7. Loosen the bagels with a knife. Turn the bread on the side and slice into half.
8. Serve with toppings of your choice such as butter or cream cheese.
9. Refrigerate or freeze unused portions.

Chapter 3: Cakes

Regular Cakes
Carrot & Almond Cake

Yields Provided: 8 servings
Nutritional Macros - One Individual Serving:
- 4 g Net Carbs
- 25 g Total Fats
- 6 g Total Protein
- 268 Calories

Ingredient List:
- Eggs (3)
- Apple pie spice (1.5 tsp.)
- Almond flour (1 cup)
- Swerve (.66 cup)
- Baking powder (1 tsp.)
- Coconut oil (.25 cup)
- Shredded carrots (1 cup)
- Heavy whipping cream (.5 cup)
- Chopped walnuts (.5 cup)
- *Also Needed:* Instant Pot & Steamer rack/trivet

Preparation Steps:
1. Grease the cake pan.
2. Combine all of the fixings with the mixer until well incorporated. Pour into the pan and cover with a layer of foil.
3. Pour two cups of water into the Instant Pot bowl along with the steamer rack.
4. Arrange the pan on the trivet and set the pot using the cake button (40 min.).
5. Natural release the pressure for ten minutes, and quick release the rest of the built-up pressure.
6. Place on a rack to cool before frosting. You can also eat it plain.

Chocolate & Zucchini Cake

Yields Provided: 10 servings
Nutritional Macros - One Individual Serving:
- 7.4 g Net Carbs
- 10.1 g Total Protein
- 26.5 g Total Fats
- 306 Calories

Ingredient List:
- Almond flour (3 cups)
- Baking soda (1 tsp.)
- Coconut flour (.25 cup)
- Cacao powder (.5 cup)
- Eggs (4)
- Vanilla extract (3 tsp.)
- Apple cider vinegar (1 tbsp.)
- Melted cacao butter (.25 cup)
- Coconut cream (.75 cup
- Grated zucchini (2 cups)
- Erythritol, birch xylitol, or a blend such as Lakanto (6 tbsp.)
- Salt (1 pinch)
- *Also Needed:* 8x8 cake pan

Preparation Steps:
1. Heat the oven in advance until it reaches 350° Fahrenheit.
2. Prepare the pan with baking paper or a spritz of coconut oil or ghee.
3. Combine the dry components and toss with the rest fixings until combined.
4. Dump the batter into the cake tin.
5. Bake until it is no longer wobbly in the middle (for 30 to 40 min.).
6. Cool completely and serve plain or with whipped coconut cream, berries or a simple chocolate glaze.

Chocolate Lava Cake

Yields Provided: 4 servings
Nutritional Macros - One Individual Serving:
- 3 g Net Carbs
- 17 g Total Fats
- 8 g Total Protein
- 189 Calories

Ingredient List:
- Unsweetened cocoa powder (.5 cup)
- Melted butter (.25 cup)
- Eggs (4)
- Sugar-free chocolate sauce (.25 cup)
- Sea salt (.5 tsp.)
- Ground cinnamon (.5 tsp.)
- Pure vanilla extract (1 tsp.)
- Stevia (.25 cup)
- *Also Needed:* Ice cube tray or 4 ramekins

Preparation Steps:
1. Pour 1 tablespoon of the chocolate sauce into 4 of the tray slots and freeze.
2. Warm up the oven to 350° Fahrenheit.
3. Lightly grease the ramekins with butter or a spritz of oil.
4. Mix the salt, cinnamon, cocoa powder, and stevia until combined. Whisk in each of the eggs. Stir in the melted butter and vanilla.
5. Fill each of the ramekins halfway and add one of the frozen chocolates. Cover the rest of the container with the cake batter.
6. Bake for 13-14 minutes. When they're set, place on a rack to cool for about five minutes. Remove and put on a serving dish.
7. Enjoy by slicing its molten center.

Glazed Pound Cake

Yields Provided: 16 servings
Nutritional Macros - One Individual Serving:
- 2.49 g Net Carbs
- 23.4 g Total Fats
- 8 g Total Protein
- 254 Calories

Ingredient List - The Cake:
- Salt (.5 tsp.)
- Almond flour (2.5 cups)
- Softened - unsalted butter (.5 cup)
- Erythritol (1.5 cups)
- Unchilled eggs (8)
- Lemon extract (.5 tsp.)
- Vanilla extract (1.5 tsp.)
- Cream cheese (8 oz.)
- Baking powder (1.5 tsp.)

Ingredient List - The Glaze:
- Powdered erythritol (.25 cup)
- Heavy whipping cream (3 tbsp.)
- Vanilla extract (.5 tsp.)

Preparation Steps:
1. Warm the oven to 350° Fahrenheit.
2. Whisk the baking powder, almond flour, and salt. Set aside.
3. Cream the erythritol, butter, and softened cream cheese chunks. Mix until smooth in a large mixing container.
4. Whisk and add the eggs with the lemon and vanilla extract. Blend with the rest of the fixings using a hand mixer until smooth.
5. Dump the batter into a loaf pan. Bake for one to two hours.
6. Prepare a glaze. Mix in the vanilla extract, powdered erythritol, and heavy whipping cream until smooth.
7. You must let the cake cool completely before adding the glaze.

Gooey Butter Cake

Yields Provided: 15 servings
Nutritional Macros - One Individual Serving:
- 3 g Net Carbs
- 6 g Protein
- 24 g Total Fats
- 268 Calories

Ingredient List - The Cake:
- Almond flour (2 cups)
- Swerve Sweetener (.5 cup)
- Unflavored whey protein powder (2 tbsp.)
- Baking powder (2 tsp.)
- Salt (.25 tsp.)
- Butter - melted (.5 cup)
- Large egg (1)
- Vanilla extract (.5 tsp.)
- *Also Needed*: 9x13 baking pan

Ingredient List - The Filling:
- Cream cheese softened (8 oz.)
- Softened butter (.5 cup)
- Powdered Swerve (.75 cup)
- Eggs (2 large)
- Vanilla extract (.5 tsp.)
- Powdered Swerve for dusting

Preparation Steps:
1. Warm up the oven ahead of baking time to reach 325° Fahrenheit.
2. Lightly grease the pan.
3. Combine the protein powder, almond flour, swerve sweetener, salt, and baking powder.
4. Stir in the butter with the egg and vanilla extract.
5. Add to the bottom and sides of the greased baking pan.
6. In a separate container, beat the butter and cream cheese together until creamy smooth. Add in the eggs, sweetener, and vanilla.
7. Pour the filling over the crust.
8. Bake until the filling is mostly set but the center still jiggles (35-45 minutes). The edges should be a light golden brown.
9. Cool and dust with powdered swerve. Cut into bars.

Orange Rum Cake

Yields Provided: 8 servings
Nutritional Macros - One Individual Serving:
- 4 g Net Carbs
- 22 g Total Fats
- 7 g Total Protein
- 262 Calories

Ingredient List:
- Eggs (3)
- Baking powder (2 tsp.)
- Almond flour (1.5 cups)
- Butter - softened (.5 cup)
- Coconut flour (.5 cup)
- Orange extract (1 tsp.)
- Xanthan gum (.25 tsp.)
- Salt (1 pinch)
- Granulated erythritol sweetener (.75 cup or as desired)
- Almond milk (1 cup)
- Gold rum (3 tbsp.)
- Orange zest (1 tsp.)
- *Also Needed:*
- Instant Pot & trivet
- Baking pan to fit inside the cooker

Preparation Steps:
1. Combine in a blender: Eggs, zest, orange extract, gold rum, almond milk, erythritol, and the butter.
2. Blend 1 minute and add the rest of the fixings (Baking powder, almond flour, xanthan gum, coconut flour, and salt). Blend an additional 20 seconds.
3. Grease the pan to fit inside the Instant Pot on the trivet. Pour in 1 cup of water and secure the lid.
4. Use the high-pressure setting (8 min.).
5. Quick-release the pressure and open the lid to cool.

Pumpkin Bread

Yields Provided: 8 servings
Nutritional Macros - One Individual Serving:
- 5 g Net Carbs
- 26 g Total Fats
- 8 g Total Protein
- 311 Calories

Ingredient List:
- Almond flour (1 cup)
- Libby's Canned Pumpkin (1 small can)
- Baking powder (.5 tsp.)
- Coconut flour (.5 cup)
- Heavy cream (.5 cup)
- Stevia (.5 cup)
- Melted butter (1 stick)
- Large eggs (4)
- Vanilla (1.5 tsp.)
- Pumpkin spice (2 tsp.)

Preparation Steps:
1. Set the oven temperature setting to 350° Fahrenheit. Grease a pie plate with a spritz of coconut oil.
2. Mix the fixings in a bowl until light and fluffy.
3. Dump the batter into the prepared pie plate.
4. Bake for 70 to 90 minutes.

Slow-Cooked Raspberry Coconut Cake

Yields Provided: 10 servings
Nutritional Macros - One Individual Serving:
- 7 g Net Carbs
- 10 g Total Protein
- 32 g Total Fats
- 362 Calories

Ingredient List:
- Almond flour (2 cups)
- Swerve sweetener (.75- 1 cup)
- Unsweetened shredded coconut (1 cup)
- Large eggs (4)
- Powdered egg whites (.25 cup)
- Salt (.25 tsp.)
- Baking soda (2 tsp.)
- Melted coconut oil (.5 cup)
- Raspberries – fresh or frozen (1 cup)
- Coconut extract (1 tsp.)
- Almond or coconut milk (.75 cup)
- Sugar-free dark chocolate chips (.33 cup)
- Coconut oil or favorite cooking spray
- *Recommended:* 6-quart size slow cooker

Preparation Steps:
1. Spritz the inside of the cooker with cooking oil spray.
2. Whisk the flour, sweetener, coconut, salt, baking soda, and powdered egg whites in a large mixing container.
3. Add the coconut or almond milk, eggs, coconut extract, and melted coconut oil. Stir well and fold in the chips and berries.
4. Spread the prepared batter into the cooker.
5. Set the timer for three hours. Chill and garnish with whipped cream and serve.

Bar Cakes
Almond Coconut Bars

Yields Provided: 6 servings
Nutritional Macros - One Individual Serving:
- 2 g Net Carbs
- 5 g Total Protein
- 25 g Total Fats
- 253 Calories

Ingredient List:
- Coconut oil (.5 cup)
- Almond flour (1.25 cups)
- Coconut flour (.25 cup
- Eggs (2)
- Sugar substitute (3 tbsp.)
- Almond butter (2 tbsp.)
- Salt (.25 tsp.)
- Water (1 cup)
- Vanilla extract (1 tsp.)
- *Also Needed:* Baking pan & Trivet for the Instant Pot

Preparation Steps:
1. Line the pan that fits in the cooker with the baking paper.
2. Combine all of the fixings in the food processor. Empty into the pan.
3. Empty the water into the Instant Pot with the steamer rack. Arrange the pan in the cooker and secure the lid.
4. Set the timer for 15 minutes.
5. Natural-release the pressure and chill the pan until its room temperature.
6. Slice into six bars.

Cheesecake Mocha Bars

Yields Provided: 16 servings
Nutritional Macros - One Individual Serving:
- 3.2 g Net Carbs
- 6.1 g Total Protein
- 21.2 g Total Fats
- 232 Calories

Ingredient List - The Brownie Layer:
- Vanilla extract (2 tsp.)
- Unsalted butter (6 tbsp.)
- Large eggs (3)
- Salt (.5 tsp.)
- Instant coffee (.5 tbsp.)
- Bak. powder (1 tsp.)
- Almond flour (1.5 cups)
- Hershey's Baking Cocoa or your favorite (.5 cup)
- Erythritol (1 cup)

Ingredient List - The Cream Cheese Layer:
- Softened cream cheese (1 lb.)
- Erythritol (.5 cup)
- Large egg (1)
- Vanilla extract (1 tsp.)
- *Also Needed:* 8x8-inch baking pan

Preparation Steps:
1. Set the oven temperature to 350° Fahrenheit.
2. Lightly grease or spray the pan.
3. Combine the wet fixings starting with the vanilla and butter. Mix in the eggs.
4. In another container, combine the dry ingredients and whisk in with the wet fixings. Set aside 1/4 cup of the batter for later. Pour the mixture into the pan.
5. Mix the room temperature cream cheese with the rest of the fixings for the second layer. Spread it on the sheet of brownies.
6. Use the reserved batter as the last layer (it will be thin). Bake for 30-35 minutes.
7. When cooled, slice the cheesecake bars, and serve or store for later.

Chocolate Peppermint Cookie Bars

Yields Provided: 10 servings
Nutritional Macros - One Individual Serving:
- 5.1 g Net Carbs
- 5 g Total Protein
- 11 g Total Fats
- 123 Calories

Ingredient List:
- Shredded coconut (3 cups)
- Granulated erythritol/monk fruit blend (2 tbsp.)
- Grass-fed ghee (2 tbsp.)
- Collagen protein (6 tbsp.)
- Food grade peppermint essential oil (4-6 drops)
- Organic chlorella powder (2 tsp.)
- Vanilla extract (3 tsp.)
- Salt (1 pinch)

Ingredient List - The Drizzle:
- Cacao powder (2 tbsp.)
- Melted ghee or coconut oil (3 tbsp.)
- Vanilla extract (1 tsp.)
- Granulated erythritol/monk fruit blend (1 tbsp.) or 15 drops liquid stevia

Preparation Steps:
1. Prepare the cookie bars first. Toss the coconut into the blender and mix using the medium to high speed until finely chopped.
2. Add the remaining cookie bar ingredients except for the collagen. Blend until well combined.
3. Add the collagen and mix using the lowest speed until just incorporated to avoid damaging the proteins.
4. Prepare the pan with parchment, and scoop out the ingredients into the tin.
5. Press down evenly with a spoon and freeze until they are firm enough to slice (40-60 minutes).
6. While the cookie bars set, prepare the chocolate drizzle in a small bowl.
7. Remove the bars carefully from the pan and slice. Run your knife under hot water and work slowly for best results.
8. Drizzle the sliced cookie bars with the chocolate mixture and freeze for at least five more minutes.
9. Serve cold and store in the freezer.

Coconut Bars

Yields Provided: 20 servings
Nutritional Macros - One Individual Serving:
- 2 g Net Carbs
- 2 g Total Protein
- 11 g Total Fats
- 108 Calories

Ingredient List:
- Unsweetened shredded coconut (3 cups)
- Coconut oil (1 cup)
- Liquid sweetener of choice (.25 cup)

Preparation Steps:
1. Prepare a pan with a layer of parchment baking paper.
2. Combine the ingredients to make a thick batter.
3. Pour into the pan and freeze until firm.
4. Cut into squares and store until you want a delicious snack.

Keto Magic Bars

Yields Provided: 16 servings
Nutritional Macros - One Individual Serving:
- 4.5 g Net Carbs
- 2 g Total Protein
- 12.4 g Total Fats
- 132 Calories

Ingredient List:
- Almond flour (1.5 cups)
- Sweetener of choice or stevia equivalent (2 tbsp.)
- Melted coconut oil (3 tbsp.)
- Salt (.25 tsp.)
- Mini chocolate chips or sugar-free chocolate chips (.75 cup)
- Full-fat shredded coconut (.66 cup)
- Full-fat canned coconut milk (1.25 cup)
- *Optional*: Finely chopped walnuts (.25 cup)
- *Optional*: Cocoa powder (2 tbsp.)

Preparation Steps:
1. Prepare a baking pan with a layer of parchment baking paper.
2. Toss the salt, sweetener, almond flour, and oil together in the mixing bowl.
3. Press the mixture into the pan.
4. Toss the coconut, chips of chocolate, and nuts over the top.
5. Stir together the cocoa with the coconut milk. Pour this over the top.
6. Bake for 33 minutes.
7. Transfer the bars from the oven.
8. Cool for about 15 minutes to firm up.
9. Slice into bars, wiping the knife after each cut.
10. Refrigerate the bars overnight to make them more firm.

Mixed Berry Cake Bars

Yields Provided: 12 servings
Nutritional Macros - One Individual Serving:
- 3.3 g Net Carbs
- 7.0 g Total Protein
- 14 g Total Fats
- 169 Calories

Ingredient List:
   Mixed berries - fresh or frozen (1.5 cups)

Ingredient List - Wet Fixings:
- Melted - unsalted butter or refined coconut oil (4 tbsp.)
- Eggs (5)
- Lemon juice (1 tbsp.)
- Unsweetened almond milk (.33 cup)
- Apple cider vinegar (1 tbsp.)
- Vanilla (1 tsp.)
- Stevia powder (.25 tsp.)

Ingredient List - Dry Fixings:
- Blanched almond flour (1.5 cups)
- Stevia powder (1 tsp.)
- Coconut flour (6 tbsp.)
- Bak. powder (1 tsp.)
- Psyllium husk powder (1 tbsp.)
- Salt (.5 tsp.)
- Bak. soda (.5 tsp.)
- *Also Needed:* 9x13-inch baking pan

Preparation Steps:
1. Warm up the oven to 350° Fahrenheit.
2. Place a layer of baking paper in the pan.
3. Combine the wet fixings in a bowl and let sit for a couple of minutes
4. Whisk the dry components in another container.
5. Combine everything with the spatula. Let the mixture sit for a minute for the psyllium husk powder and coconut flour to absorb the liquid.
6. Fold in the berries and mix.
7. Add the batter to the pan.
8. Bake for approximately 35 minutes.
9. Check with a cake tester for doneness. If needed, bake for another five minutes.

Peanut Butter Protein Bars

Yields Provided: 12 servings
Nutritional Macros - One Individual Serving:
- 3 g Net Carbs
- 7 g Total Protein
- 14 g Total Fats
- 172 Calories

Ingredient List:
- Almond meal (1.5 cups)
- Keto-friendly chunky peanut butter (1 cup)
- Egg whites (2)
- Almonds (.5 cup)
- Cashews (.5 cup)

Preparation Steps:
1. Heat the oven ahead of time to reach 350° Fahrenheit.
2. Spritz a baking dish lightly with coconut or olive oil.
3. Combine all of the fixings and add to the prepared dish.
4. Bake for 15 minutes and cut into 12 pieces once they're cool.
5. Store in the refrigerator to keep them fresh.

Cupcakes & Mug Cakes

Blueberry Cupcakes

Yields Provided: 12 servings
Nutritional Macros - One Individual Serving:
- 2.8 g Net Carbs
- 4.4 g Total Protein
- 11.4 g Total Fats
- 138 Calories

Ingredient List:
- Melted butter (1 stick)
- Coconut flour (.5 cup)
- Granulated sweetener of choice (4 tbsp.)
- Baking powder (1 tsp.)
- Lemon juice (2 tbsp.)
- Vanilla (1 tsp.)
- Zest of a lemon (2 tbsp.)
- Eggs (8 medium)
- Fresh blueberries (1 cup)
- *Also Needed:* 12-cupcake holder and liners

Preparation Steps:
1. Set the oven temperature to 350° Fahrenheit.
2. Mix the melted butter, sweetener, coconut flour, baking powder, vanilla, lemon juice, and zest together.
3. Whisk the eggs, adding them in one at a time. Mix well.
4. Taste the cupcake batter to ensure you have used enough sweetener and flavors to mask the subtle taste of coconut from the coconut flour.
5. Pour the batter into the tins.
6. Press in a few fresh blueberries in the batter of each cupcake.
7. Pop into the oven to bake until golden brown or about 15 minutes.
8. Cover with sugar-free cream cheese frosting. Vanilla or lemon flavor is perfect. Garnish with fresh blueberries and lemon zest.
9. *Note*: Icing/frosting is additional and optional.

Brownie Mug Cake - Instant Pot

Yields Provided: 1 serving
Nutritional Macros - One Individual Serving:
- 1.3 g Net Carbs
- 9 g Total Protein
- 12 g Total Fats
- 143 Calories

Ingredient List:
- Whisked egg (1)
- Almond flour (.25 cup)
- Baking powder (.25 tsp.)
- Vanilla extract (.25 tsp.)
- Cacao powder (1.5 tbsp.)
- Cinnamon powder (1 tsp.)
- Stevia powder (2 tbsp.)
- Salt (1 pinch)

Preparation Steps:
1. Pour one cup of water and the trivet or steam rack into the Instant Pot.
2. Mix all of the fixings until well combined and pour into a mug.
3. Cover with a piece of foil and place on the rack.
4. Secure the top.
5. Set the timer for 10 minutes using the 'steam' button. Natural release the pressure (10 min.).
6. Cool a minute and enjoy.

Chocolate Mug Cake

Yields Provided: 1 serving
Nutritional Macros - One Individual Serving:
- 5 g Net Carbs
- 9 g Total Protein
- 22 g Total Fats
- 281 Calories

Ingredient List:
- Coconut flour (2 tbsp.)
- Cocoa powder - unsweetened (1 tbsp.)
- Large egg (1)
- Almond or coconut milk (2 tbsp.)
- Stevia liquid extract (10 drops)
- Coconut oil (1 tbsp.)
- Vanilla extract (.5 tsp.)
- Monk fruit liquid (10 drops)
- *Optional*: Sugar-free whipped cream
- *Optional:* Sugar-free chocolate chips (1 tbsp.)
- *Also Needed:* 1 ramekin or coffee mug

Preparation Steps:
1. Whisk the coconut flour and cocoa powder in the mug.
2. Stir in the almond milk, egg, avocado oil, vanilla extract, and sweeteners until well combined. Toss in the chocolate chips if desired.
3. Microwave using the high setting for 1.5 to 2 minutes.
4. Cool slightly and garnish with a portion of whipped cream and chocolate chips.

Pumpkin Spice Cupcakes

Yields Provided: 6 servings
Nutritional Macros - One Individual Serving:
- 3 g Net Carbs
- 2 g Total Protein
- 4 g Total Fats
- 70 Calories

Ingredient List:
- Coconut flour (3 tbsp.)
- Bak. powder (.25 tsp.)
- Salt (1 pinch)
- Bak. soda (.25 tsp.)
- Pumpkin pie spice (1 tsp.)
- Large egg (1)
- Pumpkin puree (.75 cup)
- Swerve Granular/Swerve Brown (.33 cup)
- Heavy whipping cream (.25 cup)
- Vanilla (.5 tsp.)
- *Also Needed:* 6 muffin holders & parchment or silicone liners

Preparation Steps:
1. Warm up the oven in advance to reach 350° Fahrenheit.
2. Prepare the baking pan.
3. Sift or whisk the coconut flour, pumpkin pie spice, baking powder, baking soda, and salt.
4. Use a separate container to mix the cream, sweetener, vanilla, pumpkin puree, and egg. Whisk the mixture until well combined, and fold in the remainder of dry fixings. If the batter is too thin, whisk in an additional tablespoon of coconut flour.
5. Portion into the muffin tins.
6. Bake until just puffed and barely set (25 to 30 min.).
7. Transfer the pan to the countertop (in the pan) to cool.
8. Store in the fridge for a minimum of one hour before it's time to serve.
9. Top it off using a generous helping of whipped cream.
10. *Note:* They will sink when you let them cook. It will be that much tastier with the serving of whipped cream!

Sour Cream Vanilla Cupcakes

Yields Provided: 12 servings
Nutritional Macros - One Individual Serving:
- 2 g Net Carbs
- 1 g Total Fats
- 4 g Total Protein
- 128 Calories

Ingredient List:
- Butter (4 tbsp.)
- Swerve or your favorite sweetener (1.5 cups)
- Salt (.25 tsp.)
- Eggs (4)
- Sour cream (.25 cup)
- Vanilla (1 tsp.)
- Almond flour (1 cup)
- Bak. powder (1 tsp.)
- Coconut flour (.25 cup)
- Also Needed: Muffin tins

Preparation Steps:
1. Heat the oven to reach 350° Fahrenheit.
2. Prepare the butter and sweetener until creamy and fluffy using the mixer.
3. Blend in the vanilla and sour cream. Mix well.
4. One at a time, fold in the eggs.
5. Sift and blend in both types of flour, salt, and baking powder.
6. Pour the batter into the cups.
7. Bake for 20 to 25 min.
8. Cool completely. Place in the fridge for fresher storage results.

Vanilla Berry Mug Cake

Yields Provided: 1 serving
Nutritional Macros - One Individual Serving:
- 4.5 g Net Carbs
- 27 g Total Fats
- 9 g Total Protein
- 342 Calories

Ingredient List:
- Baking powder (.25 tsp.)
- Melted butter (1 tbsp.)
- Cream cheese - full-fat (2 tbsp.)
- Coconut flour (2 tbsp.)
- Swerve granulated sweetener (1 tbsp.)
- Vanilla extract (1 tsp.)
- Medium egg (1)
- Frozen raspberries (6)

Preparation Steps:
1. Toss the butter and cream cheese into a coffee mug. Microwave using the high-power setting for 20 seconds.
2. Whisk the sweetener, baking powder, coconut flour, vanilla, and egg.
3. Press six whole raspberries into the batter.
4. Microwave using the high setting (1 min.20 sec.). Watch closely after 1 minute.

Zucchini Spiced Cupcakes

Yields Provided: 12 servings
Nutritional Macros - One Individual Serving:
- 3.5 g Net Carbs
- 23.1 g Total Fats
- 4.9 g Total Protein
- 68 Calories

Ingredient List - The Cakes:
- Almond flour (1 cup)
- Coconut flour (.33 - .5 cup)
- Xanthan gum (.5 tsp.)
- Bak. soda (1 tsp.)
- Bak. powder (.5 tsp.)
- Salt (.5 tsp.)
- Cinnamon (1 tsp.)
- Ground cloves (.125 tsp.)
- Nutmeg (.25 tsp.)
- Coconut oil liquified (.5 cup)
- Large eggs (2 unchilled)
- Sugar-free vanilla extract (1.5 tsp.)
- Monk fruit sweetener (1 cup)
- Packed grated zucchini (1.5 cups)
- *Optional:* Walnuts coarsely chopped

Ingredient List - The Frosting:
- Softened cream cheese (4 oz.)
- Butter (2 tbsp. softened)
- Monk fruit sweetener - powdered (.5 cup)
- Vanilla extract (.5 tsp.)
- *Also Needed*: Electric mixer or food processor

Preparation Steps:
1. Warm the oven in advance to reach 350° Fahrenheit.
2. Sift both flours together. Prepare the muffin tins with paper or foil baking liners.
3. Stir in both types of flour with the baking soda, xanthan gum, baking powder, nutmeg, cinnamon, salt, and cloves. Set aside for now.
4. Whisk the coconut oil, eggs, and vanilla extract. Stir in zucchini and sweetener, and the flour mixture. Fold in the walnuts. Add the batter to the liners.
5. Bake until the cake is firm to touch (25-30 min.).
6. Remove cool on a rack. Frost with cream cheese frosting if desired.
7. Store cupcakes in refrigerator or freezer.
8. Cool to reach room temperature before serving.

Preparation Steps - The Frosting:
1. Pour the sweetener in a blender.
2. Mix the butter and cream cheese until fully incorporated.
3. Add the vanilla and frost the cake.

Chapter 4: Fat Bombs & Pies

Blackberry Coconut Fat Bombs

Yields Provided: 16 servings
Nutritional Macros - One Individual Serving:
- 3 g Net Carbs
- 1.1 g Total Protein
- 19 g Total Fats
- 170 Calories

Ingredient List:
- Coconut oil (1 cup)
- Fresh or frozen blackberries (.5 cup)
- Coconut butter (1 cup)
- Vanilla extracts (.5 tsp.)
- Stevia drops (as desired)
- Lemon juice (1 tbsp.)
- *Also Needed:* 6x6 container

Preparation Steps:
1. Add the coconut oil, coconut butter, and frozen berries in a cooking pot using the medium heat setting.
2. Prepare a baking pan with a sheet of parchment baking paper.
3. Use a small blender and add the mixture along with the rest of the components in the recipe. Spread it out on the prepared pan. Place the bombs in the fridge for about one hour.
4. *Note*: If you use fresh berries, you won't need to cook them with the butter and coconut oil (step 1).

Blueberry Fat Bombs

Yields Provided: 24 servings
Nutritional Macros - One Individual Serving:
- 1.02 g Net Carbs
- .44 g Total Protein
- 13 g Total Fats
- 116 Calories

Ingredient List:
- Scant blueberries (1 cup)
- Butter (1 stick)
- Coconut oil (.75 cup)
- Softened cream cheese (4 oz.)
- Coconut cream (.25 cup)
- Sweetener of choice (to taste)

Preparation Steps:
1. Arrange three to four berries in each mold cup.
2. Melt the butter with the coconut oil over the lowest stovetop heat setting. Cool slightly for approximately five minutes.
3. Combine all of the ingredients and whisk well. Slowly, add the sweetener.
4. Using a spouted pitcher, fill an ice tray with 24 bombs.
5. Pop them out and eat when hunger strikes.

Cheesecake Surprise Fat Bombs

Yields Provided: 12 servings
Nutritional Macros - One Individual Serving:
- 1 g Net Carbs
- 6.5 g Total Fats
- 1 g Total Protein
- 120 Calories

Ingredient List:
- Creamy - keto-friendly peanut butter (2 oz. or .25 cup)
- Cream cheese (4 oz.)
- Swerve granular sweetener (2 tbsp.)
- *Optional*: Dark chocolate chips (.5 cup crushed)

Preparation Steps:
1. Let the peanut butter and cream cheese set out to room temperature before beginning the prep.
2. Whisk the ingredients together.
3. Scoop out 12 balls and roll into the chips of chocolate.
4. Place the bombs on a layer of parchment paper.
5. Freeze until solid (2 hrs.) and store in a freezer bag or other airtight container.

Chocolate Chip Cookie Dough Fat Bomb

Yields Provided: 20 servings
Nutritional Macros - One Individual Serving:
- 2 g Net Carbs
- 14 g Total Fats
- 2 g Total Protein
- 139 Calories

Ingredient List:
- Cream cheese (8 oz. pkg.)
- Salted butter (.5 cup or 1 stick)
- Sweetener – swerve/erythritol (.33 cup)
- Almond butter or creamy peanut butter - only salt and peanuts (.5 cup)
- Vanilla extract (1 tsp.)
- Baking chips - stevia-sweetened chocolate chips (4 oz.)

Preparation Steps:
1. Remove the cream cheese from the fridge for about 20 to 30 minutes to soften.
2. Use a mixer to blend all of the fixings. Refrigerate for at least 30 minutes before adding them onto a tray lined with a layer of parchment paper.
3. Spray an ice cream scoop with a spritz of cooking spray (preferably coconut oil).
4. Scoop out 20 bomb portions and place them onto the baking pan.
5. Freeze for a minimum of 30 minutes.
6. Store in the fridge in a zipper-type plastic bag for convenience.

Cocoa Butter Walnut Fat Bombs

Yields Provided: 8 servings
Nutritional Macros - One Individual Serving:
- 0.3 g Net Carbs
- 0.9 g Total Protein
- 20 g Total Fats
- 265 Calories

Ingredient List:
- Coconut oil (4 tbsp.)
- Erythritol (4 tbsp. powdered)
- Butter (4 tbsp.)
- Cocoa butter (4 oz.)
- Chopped walnuts (.5 cup)
- Vanilla extract (.5 tsp.)
- Salt (.25 tsp)

Preparation Steps:
1. Prepare a pan using the medium-high temperature setting on the stovetop. Add the butter, coconut oil, and cocoa butter.
2. Once it's melted, add the walnuts, salt, stevia, vanilla extract, and erythritol. Mix well.
3. Pour into the silicone mold. Store the treats in the refrigerator for one hour before serving.

Coconut Macaroon Fat Bombs

Yields Provided: 10 servings
Nutritional Macros - One Individual Serving:
- 0.5 g Net Carbs
- 1.8 g Total Protein
- 5 g Total Fats
- 46 Calories

Ingredient List:
- Shredded coconut (.5 cup)
- Organic almond flour (.25 cup)
- Swerve (2 tbsp.)
- Coconut oil (1 tbsp.)
- Egg whites (3)
- Vanilla extract (1 tbsp.)

Preparation Steps:
1. In a mixing bowl, blend the swerve, coconut, and almond flour until well combined.
2. Warm the oil in a saucepan and stir in the vanilla extract.
3. Place a medium-sized bowl in the freezer.
4. Combine the oil into the flour mixture, mixing well.
5. Put the whites of the eggs into the cold dish and whisk until stiff – foamy peaks are formed. Fold in the whites with the flour.
6. Scoop the mixture into the muffin cups.
7. Bake until the macaroons are lightly browned or about eight minutes.
8. Cool before placing on a serving dish or store for later.

Coconut Orange Creamsicle Fat Bombs

Yields Provided: 10 servings
Nutritional Macros - One Individual Serving:
- .95 g Net Carbs
- 1.04 g Total Protein
- 19 g Total Fats
- 177 Calories

Ingredient List:
- Coconut oil (.5 cup)
- Heavy whipping cream (.5 cup)
- Cream cheese (4 oz.)
- Orange Vanilla Mio (1 tsp.)
- Liquid stevia (10 drops)
- Also Needed: Immersion blender & Silicone tray

Preparation Steps:
1. Blend all of the ingredients together. If the mixture is too stiff, microwave it for a couple of seconds.
2. Spread the fixings into the tray and freeze for about two to three hours.
3. Once it's hardened, transfer to a container and store in the freezer until desired.

Coffee Fat Bombs

Yields Provided: 15 servings
Nutritional Macros - One Individual Serving:
- 0 g Net Carbs
- 4 g Total Fats
- 0 g Total Protein
- 45 Calories

Ingredient List:
- Unchilled cream cheese (4.4 oz.)
- Instant coffee (1 tbsp.)
- Powdered xylitol (2 tbsp.)
- Unsweetened cocoa powder (1 tbsp.)
- Coconut oil (1 tbsp.)
- Unchilled butter (1 tbsp.)

Preparation Steps:
1. With a blender/food processor, blitz the xylitol and coffee into a fine powder. Add the hot water to form a pasty mix.
2. Blend in the cream cheese, butter, cocoa powder, and coconut oil.
3. Add to ice cube trays and freeze a minimum of one to two hours.
4. Use a zipper-type baggie to keep them fresh in the freezer.

Dark Chocolate Fat Bombs

Yields Provided: 12 servings
Nutritional Macros - One Individual Serving:
- 5.6 g Net Carbs
- 10.5 g Total Fats
- 4 g Total Protein
- 96 Calories

Ingredient List:
- Stevia extract (1 tsp.)
- Butter/coconut oil (.5 cup)
- Almond butter (.5 cup)
- Dark chocolate – 85% or higher (3 oz.)
- Sea salt (.25 tsp.)

Preparation Steps:
1. Mix all of the components in the recipe until smooth using a double boiler.
2. Empty the mixture into 12 ice trays. Freeze for at least one hour.
3. Serve when desired.

Lemon Cheesecake Fat Bombs

Yields Provided: 12 servings
Nutritional Macros - One Individual Serving:
- 1 g Net Carbs
- 1 g Total Protein
- 9 g Total Fats
- 80 Calories

Ingredient List:
- Coconut oil (.25 cup)
- Unsalted butter (.25 cup)
- Cream cheese (4 oz.)
- Favorite natural sweetener (2 tbsp.)
- Fresh lemon juice (1 oz.)
- Lemon zest (1 lemon) optional
- Blueberries or your favorite berries (12)

Preparation Steps:
1. Use a hand mixer to blend the butter, coconut oil, cream cheese, and sweetener together until creamy smooth.
2. Grate and add the lemon zest and juice.
3. Toss a blueberry into each of the bombs and freeze until firm.
4. Pop each one out the molds and keep frozen in an airtight container until you need them.

Neapolitan Fat Bombs

Yields Provided: 24 servings
Nutritional Macros - One Individual Serving:
- .66 g Net Carbs
- .51 Total Protein
- 11 g Total Fats
- 103 Calories

Ingredient List:
- Butter (.5 cup)
- Coconut oil (.5 cup)
- Sour cream (.5 cup)
- Cream cheese (.5 cup)
- Erythritol (2 tbsp.)
- Liquid stevia (25 drops)
- Cocoa powder (2 tbsp.)
- Strawberries (2 medium)
- Vanilla extract (1 tsp.)
- *Also Needed: I*mmersion blender

Preparation Steps:
1. Combine each of the fixings except for the strawberries, cocoa, and vanilla. Mix with the immersion blender.
2. Divide the mixture into three dishes; adding the vanilla in one, cocoa in one, and the berries in the last dish.
3. Pour the chocolate powder into the mold and freeze for about 30 minutes. Continue the process with the vanilla layer (30 min.) and the strawberry layer.
4. Freeze together for at least one hour.

Orange & Walnut Chocolate Fat Bombs

Yields Provided: 8 servings
Nutritional Macros - One Individual Serving:
- 2 g Net Carbs
- 9 g Total Fats
- 1 g Total Protein
- 87 Calories

Ingredient List:
- 85% Cocoa dark chocolate (12.5 grams)
- Extra-Virgin coconut oil (.25 cup)
- Orange peel or orange extract (.5 tbsp.)
- Walnuts (1.75 cups)
- Cinnamon (1 tsp.)
- Stevia (10-15 drops)

Preparation Steps:
1. Use the microwave or a saucepan to melt the chocolate. Add cinnamon and coconut oil. Sweeten mixture with stevia.
2. Pour in the fresh orange peel and chopped walnuts.
3. In a muffin tin or in candy mold, spoon in the mixture.
4. Place in the refrigerator for one to three hours until the mixture is solid.

Peppermint & Chocolate Fat Bombs

Yields Provided: 6 servings
Nutritional Macros - One Individual Serving:
- 1.1 g Net Carbs
- 21.1 g Total Fats
- 0.4 g Total Protein
- 188 Calories

Ingredient List:
- Melted coconut oil (4.5 oz.)
- Granulated sweetener - your choice (1 tbsp.)
- Unsweetened coconut (2 tbsp.)
- Peppermint essence (.25 tsp.)

Preparation Steps:
1. Combine the coconut oil, sweetener, and peppermint essence.
2. Pour about half of the bomb mixture into a six-count ice cube tray. Let them stay in the fridge for a white layer.
3. Use the remainder of the mixture to blend in with the cocoa powder.
4. Empty the chocolate mix on top of the trays.
5. Place it back into the fridge until firm. Pop it out and eat.

Stuffed Pecan Fat Bombs

Yields Provided: 1 serving
Nutritional Macros - One Individual Serving:
- 2 g Net Carbs
- 31 g Total Fats
- 11 g Total Protein
- 150 Calories

Ingredient List:
- Pecan halves (4)
- Coconut butter/unsalted butter (.5 tbsp.)
- Cream cheese (1 oz.)
- Your favorite flavor mix – herb or veggie
- Sea salt (1 pinch)

Preparation Steps:
1. Warm up the oven to 350° Fahrenheit. Once it's hot, toast the pecans for 8 to 10 minutes and cool.
2. Let the cream cheese and butter soften. Add the mixture with your favorite flavored mix, veggie, or herbs. Mix until smooth.
3. Spread the tasty fixings between the two pecan halves.
4. Drizzle with some sea salt and serve.

Pies

Creamy Lime Pie

Yields Provided: 8 servings
Nutritional Macros - One Individual Serving:
- 4.2 g Net Carbs
- 7 g Total Protein
- 38.6 g Total Fats
- 386 Calories

Ingredient List:
- Almond flour (1.5 cups)
- Erythritol (divided - .5 cup)
- Salt (.5 tsp.)
- Melted butter (.25 cup)
- Heavy cream (1 cup)
- Egg yolks (4)
- Freshly squeezed key lime juice (.33 cup)
- Lime zest (1 tbsp.)
- Cubed cold butter (.25 cup)
- Vanilla extract (1 tsp.)
- Xanthan gum (.25 tsp.)
- Sour cream (1 cup)
- Cream cheese (.5 cup)

Preparation Steps:
1. Warm up the oven to 350° Fahrenheit.
2. Melt the butter in a pan.
3. Mix the salt, half or .25 cup of the erythritol, and the almond flour. Slowly add the butter. Blend and press into a pie platter.
4. Bake for 15 minutes. Remove when it's lightly browned. Let it cool.
5. In another saucepan, combine the egg yolks, heavy cream, rest of the erythritol, lime zest, and juice.
6. Simmer using the medium heat temperature setting until it starts to thicken (7-10 min.).
7. Take the pan from the heat and add the xanthan gum, vanilla extract, cold butter, cream cheese, and sour cream. Whisk until smooth.
8. Scoop into the cooled pie shell. Cover and place in the fridge.
9. *Note:* You can serve after four hours but it is better if you wait overnight to enjoy the delicious treat.

Pumpkin Cheesecake Pie

Yields Provided: 8 servings
Nutritional Macros - One Individual Serving:
- 6 g Net Carbs
- 10 g Total Protein
- 44 g Total Fats
- 460 Calories

Ingredient List:
- Almond flour (1.75 cups)
- Cinnamon (.5 tsp.)
- Swerve (3 tbsp.)
- Melted butter (1 stick)

Ingredient List - The Filling:
- Pumpkin puree (.66 cup)
- Swerve (.66 cup)
- Vanilla extract (.5 tsp.)
- Cinnamon (.5 tsp.)
- Nutmeg (.25 tsp.)
- Allspice (.125 tsp.)
- Unchilled large eggs (2)
- Unchilled cream cheese (16 oz.)
- *Also Needed*: (1) 9-inch pie plate

Preparation Steps:
1. Prepare the crust. Combine the cinnamon, sweetener, and almond flour in the baking dish. Melt and stir in the butter. Press the fixings together.
2. Prepare the filling. Mix the sweetener, vanilla, and cream cheese with an electric mixer. When smooth blend in the pumpkin, nutmeg, eggs, cinnamon, and allspice.
3. Scrape the filling into the crust. Bake for 35-40 minutes. Remove when the filling is firm.
4. Set aside to cool down on a wire rack. Chill overnight or for at least a few hours before serving in equal portions.

Sour Cream Lemon Pie

Yields Provided: 10 servings
Nutritional Macros - One Individual Serving:
- 3.9 g Net Carbs
- 5.8 g Protein
- 31.1 g Total Fats
- 330 Calories

Ingredient List:
- Press-in pie crust baked (see below - 1 recipe)
- Heavy cream (1 cup)
- Egg yolks (4 large)
- Lemon juice (.33 cup)
- Lemon zest (1 tbsp.)
- Butter chilled & cut into pieces (.25 cup)
- Lemon extract (1 tsp.)
- Xanthan gum (.25 tsp.)
- Powdered Swerve Sweetener (.5 to .75 cup)
- Full-fat sour cream (1 cup)

Preparation Steps:
1. Dice the butter into small pieces and keep chilled until ready to use.
2. Use the medium heat setting and add the fixings into the pan (the cream, egg yolks, lemon juice, and lemon zest).
3. Simmer, stirring often until the mixture thickens (5-8 min.).
4. Transfer the pan to the countertop. Stir in the lemon extract, butter, xanthan gum, and sweetener (as desired). Whisk in the sour cream until it's lump-free.
5. Empty the filling into the pie shell and refrigerate for a minimum of four hours to set. Overnight is the best; so, just pop into the freezer for an hour after being refrigerated.
6. Top with lightly sweetened whipped cream.
7. *Note:* Carbs from the crust are included.

Low-Carb Almond Flour Crust

Yields Provided: 10 servings
Nutritional Macros - One Individual Serving:
- 1.8 g Net Carbs
- 3.7 g Total Protein
- 12.7 g Total Fats
- 187 Calories

Ingredient List:
- Almond flour (1.5 cups)
- Swerve Sweetener - powdered or granular (.25 cup)
- Salt (.25 tsp.)
- Melted butter (.25 cup)

Preparation Steps:
1. Whisk the sweetener with the salt and almond flour.
2. Stir in the melted butter to form a crumbly dough.
3. Turn out into the pie plate and firmly press. Use a fork to prick the crust all over before baking.
4. To bake unfilled, warm up the oven to reach 325° Fahrenheit. Bake until the edges are golden brown (20 min.)
5. To bake a filled pie, bake for about ten to twelve minutes before adding the filling. You may need to cover the edges in foil to avoid over-browning.
6. *Cooking Tip*: For a savory pie crust, leave out the sweetener, use .5 tsp. of salt, and add .5 tsp. of garlic powder.

Mini Coconut Pies

Yields Provided: 12 servings
Nutritional Macros - One Individual Serving:
- 3 g Net Carbs
- 3 g Total Protein
- 13 g Total Fats
- 174 Calories

Ingredient List:
- Coconut oil (1 tbsp.)
- Coconut flour (1 cup)
- Large eggs (2)
- Melted ghee (.5 cup)
- Sugar-free vanilla bean sweetener (3 tbsp.)
- Unsweetened coconut cream (1 cup)
- Unsweetened shredded coconut (.25 cup)
- *Also Needed*: 12-count mini muffin tin

Preparation Steps:
1. Heat the oven in advance to 350° Fahrenheit.
2. Lightly grease the cups of the tin with a spritz of coconut oil.
3. Whisk the eggs, ghee, coconut flour, and 1 tablespoon of the vanilla bean sweetener in a mixing container.
4. Empty the batter into the prepared muffin tins. Bake for 10 minutes.
5. Cool and remove the shells from the muffin tin.
6. Combine the shredded coconut, coconut cream, and the rest of the sweetener.
7. Top each pie shell with about 1 one tablespoon of the cream mixture. Place in the fridge for about half an hour.
8. Garnish with a portion of toasted coconut to your liking before serving.

Chapter 5: Delicious Mousse & Pudding Options

Cheesecake Pudding

Yields Provided: 4 servings
Nutritional Macros - One Individual Serving:
- 5 g Net Carbs
- 36 g Total Fats
- 5 g Total Protein
- 356 Calories

Ingredient List:
- Cream cheese or Neufchatel cheese (1 block)
- Heavy whipping cream (.5 cup)
- Lemon juice (1 tsp.)
- Sour cream (.5 cup)
- Liquid stevia (20 drops)
- Vanilla extract (1 tsp.)

Preparation Steps:
1. Microwave the cream cheese for 30 seconds or leave on the counter to soften for a few minutes before using.
2. Whip the sour cream and whipping cream together with the mixer until soft peaks form. Combine with the rest of the fixings and whip until fluffy.
3. Portion into four dishes to chill. Place a layer of the wrap over the dish and store in the fridge.
4. When ready to eat, garnish with some berries if you like.
5. *Note:* If you add berries, be sure to add the carbs.

Chocolate & Avocado Pudding

Yields Provided: 2 servings
Nutritional Macros - One Individual Serving:
- 2 g Net Carbs
- 8 g Total Protein
- 27 g Total Fats
- 281 Calories

Ingredient List:
- Cream cheese (2 oz.)
- Ripe medium avocado (1)
- Natural sweetener – swerve (1 tsp.)
- Vanilla extract (.25 tsp.)
- Unsweetened cocoa powder (4 tbsp.)
- Pink salt (1 pinch)

Preparation Steps:
1. Combine the cream cheese with the avocado, sweetener, vanilla, cocoa powder, and salt into the blender/processor.
2. Pulse until creamy smooth.
3. Measure into fancy dessert dishes and chill for at least 30 minutes.

Cinnamon Roll Mousse In A Jar

Yields Provided: 4 servings
Nutritional Macros - One Individual Serving:
- 5.1 g Net Carbs
- 29.3 g Total Fats
- 4.6 g Total Protein
- 291 Calories

Ingredient List:
- Heavy whipping cream (.5 cup)
- Softened full-fat cream cheese (4.2 oz.)
- Powdered swerve or Erythritol (.25 cup)
- Unsalted cashew butter or almond butter (2 tbsp.)
- Cinnamon (1 tsp.)
- Sugar-free vanilla extract (.5 tsp)

Ingredient List - The Drizzle:
- Coconut butter (2 tbsp.)
- Swerve or Erythritol (1 tbsp.)
- Virgin coconut oil (1 tsp.)

Preparation Steps:
1. Combine the heavy cream and cream cheese until smooth. Toss in the rest of the fixings (sweetener to taste).
2. In another container, combine the drizzle components and place in the microwave. Using 10-second intervals, warm it up until it is syrupy.
3. Portion the mouse in the jars and drizzle with the syrup. Dust with cinnamon and serve.

Peanut Butter Mousse

Yields Provided: 4 servings
Nutritional Macros - One Individual Serving:
- 3 g Net Carbs
- 6 g Total Protein
- 27 g Total Fats
- 301 Calories

Ingredient List:
- Heavy whipping cream - more if needed to thin the mixture (.5 cup)
- Cream cheese - softened (4 oz.)
- Natural peanut butter - no sugar added (.25 cup)
- Powdered Swerve Sweetener (.25 cup)
- Vanilla extract (.5 tsp.)

Preparation Steps:
1. Whisk or whip the cream until it holds stiff peaks. Set aside.
2. In another container, mix the peanut butter and cream cheese until smooth. Mix in the sweetener and vanilla. If your peanut butter is unsalted, add a pinch of salt as well. Beat until smooth.
3. If your mixture is overly thick, add about 2 tbsp. of heavy cream to lighten it and beat until combined.
4. Gently fold the whipped cream into the mixture until no streaks remain. Spoon or pipe into little dessert glasses.
5. Add a bit of low-carbohydrate sauce on top, but add those extra carbs.

Pumpkin Custard

Yields Provided: 6 servings
Nutritional Macros - One Individual Serving:
- 3 g Net Carbs
- 5 g Total Protein
- 12 g Total Fats
- 147 Calories

Ingredient List:
- Vanilla extract (1 tsp.)
- Large eggs (4)
- Granulated stevia/erythritol blend (.5 cup)
- Sea salt (.125 tsp.)
- Pumpkin pie spice (1 tsp.)
- Unchilled butter/coconut oil/ghee (4 tbsp.)
- Canned or homemade pumpkin puree (1 tsp.)
- Super-fine almond flour (.5 cup)
- Coconut cooking oil spray or butter for the pot
- *Also Needed:* 3-4-quart Crockpot

Preparation Steps:
1. Lightly grease or spray the cooker.
2. Use a mixer to whisk the eggs – blending until smooth. Slowly, add the sweetener.
3. Blend in the vanilla extract and puree. Fold in the pie spice, salt, and almond flour. Mix everything well and add to the crockpot.
4. Secure the lid with a paper towel between the top and the fixings to absorb moisture on top of the custard.
5. Cook using the low setting.
6. When it's done, it will begin to pull away from the slow cooker and the center will be set.
7. Serve warm and top it off with garnishes as desired.

Raspberry Chia Pudding

Yields Provided: 2 servings
Nutritional Macros - One Individual Serving:
- 22.3 g Net Carbs
- 9.1 g Total Protein
- 38.8 g Total Fats
- 408 Calories

Ingredient List:
- Chia seeds (4 tbsp.)
- Raspberries (.5 cup)
- Coconut milk (1 cup)
- *Also Needed:* 2 mason jars

Preparation Steps:
1. Pour the milk and raspberries into a blender.
2. Pulse until well mixed and smooth. Pour into the jars.
3. Fold in the chia seeds and stir.
4. Secure the lid and shake.
5. Store in the fridge for at least three hours before enjoying.

White Chocolate Mousse

Yields Provided: 4 servings
Nutritional Macros - One Individual Serving:
- 2.3 g Net Carbs
- 24.8 g Total Fats
- 2.5 g Total Protein
- 261 Calories

Ingredient List:
- Whipping cream (.5 cup (+) 2 tbsp. divided)
- Powdered Swerve Sweetener (.25 cup - divided)
- Vanilla extract (.75 tsp. - divided)
- Cream cheese - softened (4 oz.)
- Cocoa butter (.5 oz. - melted and cooled)

Preparation Steps:
1. Beat .5 cup of the cream with 2 tbsp. of the sweetener and .25 teaspoon of vanilla extract until it holds stiff peaks.
2. In another mixing container, briskly mix the cream cheese with the rest of the vanilla and sweetener. Beat in the melted cocoa butter until smooth.
3. Add the remainder of the whipping cream to the mixture and beat until combined.
4. Add the cream using small increments until it's like you like it.
5. Scoop into four dessert glasses and top with a few delicious fresh berries.

Chapter 6: Frozen Desserts

Butter Pecan Ice Cream

Yields Provided: 8 servings
Nutritional Macros - One Individual Serving:
- 2 g Net Carbs
- 2 g Total Protein
- 32 g Total Fats
- 302 Calories

Ingredient List:
- Butter (.25 cup)
- Heavy cream (2 cups)
- Swerve sweetener - confectioners (.5 cup)
- Salt (.25 tsp.)
- Egg yolks (2)
- Maple extract (2 tsp.)
- Lakanto Monkfruit Maple Sweetener/sweetener of choice (1 tbsp.)
- MCT oil (1 tbsp.)
- Toasted pecans (2 tbsp.)
- *Also Needed:* 8x5 loaf pan

Preparation Steps:
1. Melt the heavy cream, butter, sweetener, and salt in a small saucepan.
2. Warm using the low-heat heat; *do not boil.*
3. Whisk the egg yolks. Mix with a spoonful of butter-cream mixture and continue with a few more spoonfuls. Gradually add in the remaining yolk into the mixture on the stovetop.
4. Continue stirring until the mixture reaches 175° Fahrenheit. (It should be thick enough to coat the back of a spoon.)
5. Pour into a dish to chill in the refrigerator for about 30 minutes.
6. Pour in the maple extract, sweetener of choice, and MCT oil.
7. Dump the mixture into an ice cream machine. Churn well, and stir in the chopped pecans.
8. Spread ice cream into a pan and freeze for two to three hours for a delicious soft serve cream.

Coconut Ice Cream

Yields Provided: 8 servings
Nutritional Macros - One Individual Serving:
- 3.5 g Net Carbs
- 3 g Total Protein
- 46 g Total Fats
- 432 Calories

Ingredient List:
- Heavy cream or coconut cream for dairy-free (2 cups)
- Salt (.125 tsp.)
- Unsweetened almond/coconut milk (2 cups)
- Inulin or erythritol - low carb sweetener (.75 cup)
- Coconut extract (.25 tsp.)
- Unsweetened flaked coconut (1.25 cups)
- *Optional*: Glycerin - helps make it scoopable (2 tbsp.)
- *Optional*: Xanthan gum (.5 tsp.)

Preparation Steps:
1. Combine each of the fixings using an electric mixer.
2. Dump the mixture into an ice cream freezer and churn to your liking according to the instructions provided by the manufacturer.

Egg-Fast Vanilla Frozen Custard

Yields Provided: 4 servings
Nutritional Macros - One Individual Serving:
- 1.5 g Net Carbs
- 31.6 g Total Fats
- 9.7 g Total Protein
- 326 Calories

Ingredient List:
- Eggs (4)
- Cream cheese (4 oz.)
- Unsalted butter (4 oz.)
- Vanilla stevia drops (.5 tsp.)**
- Monk fruit liquid extract (.25 tsp.)**
- Vanilla extract (.5 tsp.)
- Cream of tartar (.25 tsp.)

Preparation Steps:
1. Carefully separate the eggs.
2. Use the low heat setting to warm the cream cheese, yolks, and butter. Whisk often until thickened.
3. Take the pan from the burner. Stir in the vanilla and sweetener.
4. Pour in the cream of tartar with the egg whites, and whisk well until stiff.
5. Whisk the egg mixes together and empty into a freezer container with a lid. Freeze for an hour, open the container, and stir well. Place back into the freezer for about one more hour.
6. Process in an ice cream maker until desired consistency is reached.
7. **Tip*: You can use another sweetener to replace the stevia and monk fruit to acquire an equal proportion of 1/3 cup sugar equivalent.
8. Adjust the sweetness to your liking.

Peanut Butter Ice Cream

Yields Provided: 8 servings
Nutritional Macros - One Individual Serving:
- 4 g Net Carbs
- 26 g Total Fats
- 10 g Total Protein
- 378 Calories

Ingredient List:
- Peanut butter - natural organic/half creamy - half chunky (1 cup)
- Swerve (.5 cup)
- Stevia extract powder (.25 tsp.)
- *Optional:* Monk fruit powder (.25 tsp.)
- *Optional:* 1/4 cup natural whey protein (.25 cup)
- Salt (.125 tsp.)
- Unsweetened almond milk (1 cup)
- Heavy cream (1.33 cups)
- Xanthan gum (.25 tsp.)
- Vanilla extract (2 tsp.)

Preparation Steps:
1. Mix the stevia, peanut butter, salt, and monk fruit, and whey protein.
2. Whisk or blend the xanthan gum and milk.
3. Pour and mix in the vanilla and heavy cream.
4. Add the fixings to an ice cream maker and process until it's like you like it.

Pistachio Ice Cream

Yields Provided: 3 servings
Nutritional Macros - One Individual Serving:
- 16 g Net Carbs
- 6 g Total Protein
- 44 g Total Fats
- 457 Calories

Ingredient List:
- Egg yolks (2)
- Coconut milk (1.75 cups)
- Honey (1 tbsp.)
- Oil (1 tbsp.)
- Chopped pistachio nuts (5 tbsp.)
- Vanilla (1 tsp.)

Preparation Steps:
1. Whisk the milk, oil, eggs, honey, and salt in a mixing container. Place in the fridge for about one hour.
2. Roast the chopped pistachios using the medium heat setting.
3. Prepare the ice cream maker and add the mixture into the bowl.
4. About halfway through the cycle, add the pistachio nuts.
5. Serve any time for a delicious snack.

Thick Dark Chocolate Milkshake

Yields Provided: 2 servings
Nutritional Macros - One Individual Serving:
- 2.5 g Net Carbs
- 4.8 g Total Protein
- 27.1 g Total Fats
- 302 Calories

Ingredient List:
- Heavy whipping cream (6 tbsp.)
- Canned coconut milk (5 tbsp.)
- Vanilla extract (.125 tsp.)
- Unsweetened dark cocoa powder (2 tbsp.)
- Stevia sugar substitute or another sugar substitute (2 tbsp.)

Preparation Steps:
1. Use an electric mixer to prepare the cream. Once stiff peaks have formed, add in the rest of the fixings and continue mixing until stiff peaks form again.
2. Put the mixture into the freezer for about 20 minutes.
3. Take the container out of the freezer and stir. Continue the process until you have reached the desired consistency.

Smoothies

Almond & Blueberry Smoothie

Yields Provided: 2 servings
Nutritional Macros - One Individual Serving:
- 6 g Net Carbs
- 15 g Total Protein
- 25 g Total Fats
- 302 Calories

Ingredient List:
- Unsweetened almond milk (16 oz.)
- Heavy cream (4 oz.)
- Stevia (to taste)
- Whey vanilla isolate powder (1 scoop)
- Frozen unsweetened blueberries (.25 cup)

Preparation Steps:
1. Toss all of the fixings into a blender.
2. Mix until smooth.
3. Serve it up in a couple of chilled glasses.

Avocado Smoothie

Yields Provided: 1 serving
Nutritional Macros - One Individual Serving:
- 4 g Net Carbs
- 6 g Total Protein
- 58 g Total Fats
- 587 Calories

Ingredient List:
- Avocado (1)
- Ice cubes (6)
- EZ-Sweetz sweetener (6 drops)
- Unsweetened almond milk (3 oz.)
- Coconut cream (3 oz.)

Preparation Steps:
1. Use a sharp knife to cut the avocado lengthwise. Remove the seeds and the skin.
2. Toss the avocado with the rest of the fixings into the blender.
3. Toss in the ice cubes and blend until the smoothie is creamy smooth.

Avocado Mint Green Smoothie

Yields Provided: 1 serving
Nutritional Macros - One Individual Serving:
- 5 g Net Carbs
- 23 g Total Fats
- 1 g Total Protein
- 221 Calories

Ingredient List:
- Avocado (3-4 oz. or .5 of 1)
- Cilantro (3 sprigs)
- Mint leaves (5-6 large)
- Vanilla extract (.25 tsp.)
- Lime juice (1 squeeze)
- Sweetener of your choice (as desired)
- Full-fat coconut milk (.75 cup)
- Almond milk (.5 cup)
- Crushed ice (1.5 cups)

Preparation Steps:
1. Measure each of the ingredients into the blender.
2. Mix well using the low-speed setting until pureed.
3. Toss in the ice and mix. Serve in a cold mug.

Banana Bread - Blueberry Smoothie

Yields Provided: 2 servings
Nutritional Macros - One Individual Serving:
- 4.7 g Net Carbs
- 23.3 g Total Fats
- 3.1 g Total Protein
- 270 Calories

Ingredient List:
- Blueberries (.25 cup)
- Chia seeds (1 tbsp.)
- Liquid stevia (10 drops)
- MCT oil (2 tbsp.)
- Golden flaxseed meal (3 tbsp.)
- Vanilla unsweetened coconut milk (2 cups)
- Xanthan gum (.25 tsp.)
- Banana extract (1.5 tsp.)
- Ice cubes (2-3)

Preparation Steps:
1. Combine each of the fixings into a blender.
2. Wait a few minutes for the seeds and flax to absorb some of the liquid.
3. Pulse for one or two minutes until well combined.
4. Add the ice to your preference.

Blackberry Cheesecake Smoothie

Yields Provided: 1 serving
Nutritional Macros - One Individual Serving:
- 7 g Net Carbs
- 6 g Total Protein
- 53 g Total Fats
- 515 Calories

Ingredient List:
- Extra-virgin coconut oil (1 tbsp.)
- Fresh/frozen blackberries (.5 cup)
- Water (.5 cup)
- Coconut milk/heavy whipping cream (.25 cup)
- Full-fat cream cheese or creamed coconut milk (.25 cup)
- Sugar-free vanilla extract (.5 tsp.)
- Liquid stevia (3 to 5 drops as desired)

Preparation Steps:
1. Arrange all of the fixings in the blender.
2. Pulse until it's smooth and frothy.
3. Add a few ice cubes and enjoy it in a chilled glass.

Blueberry Yogurt Smoothie

Yields Provided: 2 servings
Nutritional Macros - One Individual Serving:
- 2 g Net Carbs
- 2 g Total Protein
- 5 g Total Fats
- 70 Calories

Ingredient List:
- Blueberries (10)
- Yogurt (.5 cup)
- Vanilla extract (.5 tsp.)
- Coconut milk (1 cup)
- Stevia (as desired)

Preparation Steps:
1. Add all of the fixings into a blender. Mix well.
2. When creamy smooth, pour into two chilled mugs and enjoy.

Chocolate & Cinnamon Smoothie

Yields Provided: 1 serving
Nutritional Macros - One Individual Serving:
- 14 g Net Carbs
- 3 g Total Protein
- 30 g Total Fats
- 300 Calories

Ingredient List:
- Coconut milk (.75 cup)
- Ripened avocado (.5 of 1)
- Cinnamon powder (1 tsp.)
- Unsweetened cacao powder (2 tsp.)
- Vanilla extract (.25 tsp.)
- Stevia (as desired)
- *Optional:* Coconut oil (1 tsp.) or MCT Oil (.5 tsp.)

Preparation Steps:
1. Blend all of the above fixings and combine well.
2. Pour and serve when ready.

Cinnamon Roll Smoothie

Yields Provided: 1 serving
Nutritional Macros - One Individual Serving:
- 0.6 g Net Carbs
- 26.5 g Total Protein
- 3.25 g Total Fats
- 145 Calories

Ingredient List:
- Vanilla protein powder (2 tbsp.)
- Flax meal (1 tsp.)
- Almond milk (1 cup)
- Vanilla extract (.25 tsp.)
- Sweetener (4 tsp.)
- Cinnamon (.5 tsp.)
- Ice (1 cup)

Preparation Steps:
1. Mix all of the fixings in a blender.
2. Lastly, empty the ice.
3. Blend using the high setting for 30 seconds or until thickened.

Cucumber Spinach Smoothies

Yields Provided: 2 servings
Nutritional Macros - One Individual Serving:
- 3 g Net Carbs
- 10 g Total Protein
- 32 g Total Fats
- 330 Calories

Ingredient List:
- Ice cubes (6)
- Your choice of sweetener (to taste)
- Coconut milk (.75 cup)
- MCT oil (2 tbsp.)
- Cucumber (2.5 oz.)
- Spinach (2 handfuls)
- Coconut milk (1 cup)
- Xanthan gum (.25 tsp.)

Preparation Steps:
1. Cream the coconut milk: This is a simple process. All you need to do is put the can of coconut milk in the fridge overnight. The next morning, open the can and spoon out the coconut milk that has solidified. Don't shake the can before opening. Discard the liquids.
2. Add all of the ingredients, save the ice cubes, to the blender and blend using the low speed until pureed. Thin with water as needed.
3. Add in the ice cubes and blend until the smoothie reaches your desired consistency.

Delightful Chocolate Smoothie

Yields Provided: 1 serving
Nutritional Macros - One Individual Serving:
- 4.4 g Net Carbs
- 34.5 g Total Protein
- 46 g Total Fats
- 570 Calories

Ingredient List:
- Large eggs (2)
- Extra-virgin coconut oil (1 tbsp.)
- Almond or coconut butter (1-2 tbsp.)
- Heavy whipping cream/ Coconut milk (.25 cup)
- Chia seeds (1-2 tbsp.)
- Cinnamon (.5 tsp.)
- Stevia extract (3-5 drops)
- Plain or chocolate whey protein (.25 cup)
- Unsweetened cacao powder (1 tbsp.)
- Water (.25 cup)
- Vanilla extract (.5 tsp.)
- Ice (.5 cup)

Preparation Steps:
1. Crack the eggs with the rest of fixings into a blender.
2. Pulse until frothy.
3. Add to a chilled glass and enjoy.

Mexican Chocolate Smoothie

Yields Provided: 1 serving
Nutritional Macros - One Individual Serving:
- 6 g Net Carbs
- 6 g Total Protein
- 52 g Total Fats
- 503 Calories

Ingredient List:
- Extra-virgin coconut oil (2 tbsp.)
- Chia seeds (1 tbsp.)
- Unsweetened cocoa powder (2 tbsp.)
- Coconut cream (.25 cup)
- Cayenne powder (.25 tsp.)
- Cinnamon powder (.25 tsp.)
- Organic vanilla extract (.25 tsp.)
- Water (1 cup)
- Ice cubes (3-4)

Preparation Steps:
1. Combine all of the fixings in your blender using the high-speed setting.
2. Mix until it reaches the desired consistency.

Mint Chocolate Smoothie

Yields Provided: 1 serving
Nutritional Macros - One Individual Serving:
- 6.5 g Net Carbs
- 40 g Total Fats
- 5 g Total Protein
- 401 Calories

Ingredient List:
- Medium avocado (5 of 1)
- Coconut milk (.25 cup)
- Unsweetened cashew/almond milk (1 cup)
- Swerve/erythritol (2 tbsp.)
- Cocoa powder (1 tbsp.)
- Fresh mint leaves (3-4)
- MCT oil (1 tbsp.)
- Ice cubes (2-3)
- *Optional:* Coconut milk or whipped cream

Preparation Steps:
1. Mix all of the ingredients in your blender.
2. Add ice cubes, as many as you like. Add the topping if preferred.
3. Serve.

Mocha Smoothie

Yields Provided: 3 servings
Nutritional Macros - One Individual Serving:
- 4 g Net Carbs
- 3 g Total Protein
- 16 g Total Fats
- 176 Calories

Ingredient List:
- Avocado (1)
- Coconut milk – from the can (.5 cup)
- Unsweetened almond milk (1.5 cups)
- Instant coffee crystals – regular or decaffeinated (2 tsp.)
- Vanilla extract (1 tsp.)
- Erythritol blend/granulated stevia (3 tbsp.)
- Unsweetened cocoa powder (3 tbsp.)

Preparation Steps:
1. Slice the avocado in half. Discard the pit and remove most of the center. Add it along with the rest of the fixings into a blender.
2. Mix until it's like you like it. Serve in three chilled glasses.

Pecan Pie Smoothie

Yields Provided: 1 serving
Nutritional Macros - One Individual Serving:
- 5 g Net Carbs
- 7 g Total Protein
- 36 g Total Fats

Ingredient List:
- Unsweetened almond - hemp or coconut milk (.75 cup)
- Vanilla creamer (1 tbsp.)
- Raw or lightly toasted pecans (2 tbsp.)
- Ground flax seed (2 tbsp.)
- Cashew or macadamia butter (1 tbsp.)
- Ceylon cinnamon (1 tsp.)
- Sea salt (1 dash)

Preparation Steps:
1. Toss all of the fixings into a blender and puree until creamy.
2. If you prefer a thicker smoothie, cool in the fridge for 15 to 20 minutes then serve.

Smoothie In A Bowl

Yields Provided: 1 serving
Nutritional Macros - One Individual Serving:
- 4 g Net Carbs
- 35 g Total Protein
- 35 g Total Fats
- 570 Calories

Ingredient List:
- Almond milk (.5 cup)
- Spinach (1 cup)
- Heavy cream (2 tbsp.)
- Low-carb protein powder (1 scoop)
- Coconut oil (1 tbsp.)
- Ice (2 cubes)

Ingredient List - The Toppings:
- Walnuts (4)
- Raspberries (4)
- Chia seeds 1 tsp.)
- Shredded coconut (1 tbsp.)

Preparation Steps:
1. Add a cup of spinach to your high-speed blender. Pour in the cream, almond milk, ice, and coconut oil.
2. Blend for a few seconds until it has an even consistency, and all ingredients are well combined. Empty the goodies into a serving dish.
3. Arrange your toppings or give them a toss and mix them together. Of course, you can make it pretty and alternate the strips of toppings.

Strawberry & Rhubarb Pie Smoothie

Yields Provided: 1 serving
Nutritional Macros - One Individual Serving:
- 8.6 g Net Carbs
- 14.2 g Total Protein
- 31.8 g Total Fats
- 392 Calories

Ingredient List:
- Almond butter (2 tbsp. or 1 oz. almonds)
- Medium rhubarb stalks (1.8 oz. - 1-2 stalks)
- Medium strawberries (2-4 or 1.4 oz.)
- Large organic/free-range egg (1)
- Coconut milk - full-fat cream (2 tbsp.)
- Unsweetened almond milk (.5 cup)
- Vanilla bean (1) or pure vanilla bean extract (.5 tsp.)
- Ginger root powder (.5 tsp.) or freshly grated ginger root (1 tsp.)
- Liquid stevia extract – vanilla or clear (3-6 drops)

Preparation Steps:
1. Combine each of the ingredients into a blender.
2. Pulse and enjoy when smooth.

Strawberry Smoothies

Yields Provided: 2 servings
Nutritional Macros - One Individual Serving:
- 5.1 g Net Carbs
- 18.9 g Total Protein
- 6.6 g Total Fats
- 156.8 Calories

Ingredient List:
- Almonds (8)
- Whey protein powder (1.5 scoops)
- Large strawberries (2)
- Unsweetened almond milk (16 oz.)
- Cubes of ice (6)

Preparation Steps:
1. Add all of the fixings in your blender.
2. Wait for the ice to break apart.
3. Serve in two 10-oz. chilled glasses.

Vanilla Fat-Burning Smoothie

Yields Provided: 1 serving
Nutritional Macros - One Individual Serving:
- 4 g Net Carbs
- 64 g Total Fats
- 12 g Total Protein
- 651 Calories

Ingredient List:
- Mascarpone full-fat cheese (.5 cup)
- Large egg yolks (2)
- Water (.25 cup)
- Coconut oil (1 tbsp.)
- Ice cubes (4)
- Liquid stevia (3 drops) or (1 tbsp.) powdered erythritol
- Pure vanilla extract (.5 tsp.)
- *Optional Topping:* Whipped cream

Preparation Steps:
1. Combine all of the fixings in a blender. Blend until smooth.
2. Add the whipped cream for a special treat, but add the carbs if any.

Chapter 7: Snacks

Apple Cider Donut Bites

Yields Provided: 12 servings
Nutritional Macros - One Individual Serving:
- 2.6 g Net Carbs
- 17.7 g Total Fats
- 6.5 g Total Protein
- 164 Calories

Ingredient List - The Donut Bites:
- Almond flour (2 cups)
- Swerve Sweetener (.5 cup)
- Unflavored whey protein powder (.25 cup)
- Baking powder (2 tsp.)
- Cinnamon (.5 tsp.)
- Salt (.5 tsp.)
- Large eggs (2)
- Water (.33 cup)
- Butter melted (.25 cup)
- Apple cider vinegar (1.5 tbsp.)
- Apple extract (1.5 tsp.)

Ingredient List - The Coating:
- Swerve Sweetener (.25 cup)
- Cinnamon (1-2 tsp.)
- Butter - melted (.25 cup)
- *Also Needed*: 24- count mini muffin pan

Preparation Steps:
1. Warm the oven to reach 325° Fahrenheit. Lightly grease the pan.
2. Sift the protein powder, almond flour, sweetener, baking powder, cinnamon, and salt.
3. Whisk the eggs, water, butter, apple cider vinegar, and apple extract.
4. Combine and divide the mixture among the wells of the pan.
5. Bake for 15 to 20 minutes or until the muffins are firm to the touch. Remove and let cool for 10 minutes, then transfer to a wire rack to cool completely.
6. In a small container, whisk together the sweetener and cinnamon.
7. Dip each donut bite into the melted butter, coating completely.
8. Roll each donut bite into the cinnamon/sweetener mixture.

Baked Almonds & Brie

Yields Provided: 8 servings
Nutritional Macros - One Individual Serving:
- 8 g Net Carbs
- 8.4 g Total Protein
- 12 g Total Fats
- 187 Calories

Ingredient List:
- Toasted almonds (.5 cup)
- Brie cheese (14 oz. round)
- Fresh figs (6)
- Liquid stevia (1 tbsp.)
- Water (2 tbsp.)

Preparation Steps:
1. Warm up the oven to 325° Fahrenheit.
2. Heat a saucepan of water. After hot, add the stevia and figs.
3. Simmer until softened and stir in the almonds.
4. Arrange the cheese in the baking dish. Pour the almond mixture over its top. Bake for 15 minutes.

Baked Apples

Yields Provided: 4 servings
Nutritional Macros - One Individual Serving:
- 16 g Net Carbs
- 7 g Total Protein
- 20 g Total Fats
- 175 Calories

Ingredient List:
- Keto-friendly sweetener (4 tsp. or to taste)
- Cinnamon (.75 tsp.)
- Chopped pecans (.25 cup)
- Granny Smith apples (4 large)

Preparation Steps:
1. Set the oven temperature at 375° Fahrenheit.
2. Mix the sweetener with the cinnamon and pecans.
3. Core the apple and add the prepared stuffing.
4. Add enough water into the baking dish to cover the bottom of the apple.
5. Bake for about 45 minutes to 1 hour.

Blueberry Tart

Yields Provided: 9 servings
Nutritional Macros - One Individual Serving:
- 6 g Net Carbs
- 1.1 g Total Protein
- 8.3 g Total Fats
- 103 Calories

Ingredient List:
- Blueberries (3 cups)
- Almond flour (.66 cup)
- Coconut flour (.33 cup)
- Melted butter (6 tbsp.)
- Egg (1)
- Powdered sweetener of choice (.25 cup)
- Lemon juice (1 tbsp.)

Preparation Steps:
1. Warm up the oven to reach 350° Fahrenheit.
2. Lightly grease a baking pan and add the berries with a sprinkle of lemon juice.
3. Whisk the coconut and almond flour with the sweetener and the egg.
4. Pour the mixture over the prepared berries with a drizzle of the melted butter.
5. Bake for 25 minutes.

Chocolate Coconut Bites

Yields Provided: 6 servings
Nutritional Macros - One Individual Serving:
- 9 g Net Carbs
- 9 g Total Protein
- 27 g Total Fats
- 326 Calories

Ingredient List:
- Unsweetened 80% or higher dark chocolate (4 oz.)
- Heavy cream (.33 cup)
- Coconut flour (1 cup)
- Chocolate protein powder (1 tbsp.)
- Shredded unsweetened coconut (.25 cup)
- Coconut oil (4 tbsp.)

Preparation Steps:
1. Dice the dark chocolate into bits.
2. Warm up the heavy cream in a saucepan (medium-low). Stir in the chocolate bits and oil. Continue stirring until combined, and transfer from the burner.
3. Stir in the protein powder and coconut flour. Store in the refrigerator for a minimum of two hours.
4. Take the dough out of the fridge when it's cool. Shape into balls and roll through the shredded coconut until coated.
5. Store in the fridge in a closed container.

Cinnamon Vanilla Protein Bites

Yields Provided: 18-20 bites
Nutritional Macros - One Individual Serving:
- 4 g Net Carbs
- 2 g Total Protein
- 9 g Total Fats
- 112 Calories

Ingredient List:
- Quick oats (.75 cup)
- Nut butter of choice (.25 - .33 cup)
- Cinnamon (1 tbsp.)
- Pure maple syrup (.25 - .33 cup)
- Vanilla protein powder (.25 cup)
- Almond meal (.5 cup)
- Vanilla extract (.5 - 1 tsp.)
- *Also Needed:* Food processor

Preparation Steps:
1. Line a cookie tin with a layer of parchment paper.
2. Grind the oats with the processor and add to a mixing container. Combine the cinnamon, protein powder, almond meal, and nut butter.
3. Mix in the syrup and vanilla. Using your hands, mix well and roll into small balls.
4. Freeze for 20 to 30 minutes.
5. Store in a Ziploc-type baggie with the cinnamon and vanilla protein mixture.

Cream Cheese Truffles

Yields Provided: 24 servings
Nutritional Macros - One Individual Serving:
- 2.2 g Net Carbs
- 1.2 g Total Protein
- 7 g Total Fats
- 73 Calories

Ingredient List:
- Softened cream cheese (16 oz.)
- Unsweetened cocoa powder (.5 cup - divided)
- Swerve confectioners (4 tbsp.)
- Liquid Stevia (.25 tsp.)
- Rum extract (.5 tsp.)
- Instant coffee (1 tbsp.)
- Water (2 tbsp.)
- Heavy whipping cream (1 tbsp.)
- Paper candy cups for serving (24)

Preparation Steps:
1. Combine about one-quarter of a cup of the cocoa powder with the rest of the ingredients.
2. Whisk them with an electric mixer and chill in the fridge for about 30 minutes before rolling them out.
3. Sprinkle the rest of the cocoa powder on the counter and roll out the balls (by the tablespoons) with your hands. Roll them in the powder and place them in the candy cups.
4. Chill for an additional hour before serving.

Peanut Butter & Coconut Balls

Yields Provided: 15 servings
Nutritional Macros - One Individual Serving:
- 0.92 g Net Carbs
- 0.98 g Total Protein
- 3.2 g Total Fats
- 35 Calories

Ingredient List:
- Powdered erythritol (2.5 tsp.)
- Unsweetened cocoa powder (3 tsp.)
- Creamy peanut butter – keto-friendly (3 tbsp.)
- Almond flour (2 tsp.)
- Unsweetened coconut flakes (.5 cup)

Preparation Steps:
1. Combine the peanut butter, cocoa, erythritol, and flour. Place in the freezer for one hour.
2. Spoon out a small spoon size of the peanut butter mix. Roll into the flakes until it is covered.
3. Refrigerate overnight for the best results and enjoy.

Pumpkin Blondies

Yields Provided: 12 servings
Nutritional Macros - One Individual Serving:
- 1.5 g Net Carbs
- 2 g Total Protein
- 11 g Total Fats
- 110 Calories

Ingredient List:
- Coconut oil (as needed for the pan)
- Egg (1 large)
- Softened butter (.5 cup)
- Pumpkin puree (.5 cup)
- Erythritol (.5 cup)
- Almond flour (.25 cup)
- Coconut flour (2 tbsp.)
- Cinnamon (1 tsp.)
- Pumpkin pie spice (.125 tsp.)
- Liquid stevia (15 drops)
- Maple extract (1 tsp.)
- Chopped pecans (1 oz.)

Preparation Steps:
1. Heat up the oven temperature to 350º Fahrenheit. Grease a baking pan with a spritz of coconut oil.
2. Mix the egg, butter, puree, and erythritol with an electric mixer.
3. Combine each of the flours with the pie spice, stevia, cinnamon, and maple extract.
4. Blend it all together and add to the prepared pan. Sprinkle the top with pecans.
5. Bake for 20-25 minutes until the edges are lightly browned.

Strawberries With Coconut Whip

Yields Provided: 4 servings
Nutritional Macros - One Individual Serving:
- 10 g Net Carbs
- 4 g Total Protein
- 31 g Total Fats
- 342 Calories

Ingredient List:
- Strawberries or other favorite berries (4 cups)
- Refrigerated coconut cream (2 cans)
- 70% or darker unsweetened chopped dark chocolate (1 oz.)

Preparation Steps:
1. Remove the solidified cream from the can of milk and set aside for another time; saving the liquid. Pour it into a mixing container and whip with a hand mixer until it forms stiff peaks (approximately five minutes).
2. Slice the berries and portion into four dishes. Serve with a dollop of cream. Garnish with the chopped chocolate and a few berries. Serve.

Strawberry & Cream Cakes

Yields Provided: 5 servings
Nutritional Macros - One Individual Serving:
- 3.7 g Net Carbs
- 6 g Total Protein
- 30 g Total Fats
- 275 Calories

Ingredient List:
- Eggs (3)
- Cream cheese (3 oz. / 6 tbsp.)
- Vanilla extract (.5 tsp.)
- Baking powder (.25 tsp.)
- Erythritol (2 tbsp.)

Ingredient List - The Filling:
- Strawberries (10)
- Heavy cream (1 cup)

Preparation Steps:
1. Cover a baking sheet with a layer of parchment baking paper.
2. Break the eggs and which just the egg *whites*. Whisk to form stiff peaks.
3. In another dish; combine the cream cheese, egg *yolks*, vanilla extract, baking powder, and erythritol.
4. Slowly add the egg mixture together. Shape into cake forms and place on the lined baking tin.
5. Whip the heavy cream until thickened.
6. Bake for 25 to 30 minutes.
7. Let them cool and add the berries and cream.

Strawberry Rhubarb Crumble

Yields Provided: 8 servings
Nutritional Macros - One Individual Serving:
- 3.5 g Net Carbs
- 4.2 g Total Protein
- 20.6 g Total Fats
- 230 Calories

Ingredient List - The Filling:
- Strawberries (1 cup)
- Rhubarb (1 cup)
- Lemon juice (1 tbsp.)
- Steviva Blend or your favorite stevia/erythritol baking blend (1-2 tsp)
- Xanthan gum (.5 tsp.)

Ingredient List - The Crumble:
- Walnuts (1 cup)
- Coconut flour (.5 cup)
- Flaxseed meal (.25 cup)
- Steviva Blend (or your favorite stevia/erythritol baking blend (.25 cup (+) 1 tsp.)
- Melted unsalted butter (6 tbsp.)
- Sea salt (.25 tsp.)
- *Also Needed:* 9-inch glass pie plate

Preparation Steps:
1. Finely dice the rhubarb, walnuts, and strawberries.
2. Warm up the oven to 350° Fahrenheit. Grease the pie plate with butter and set to the side for now.
3. Combine the filling ingredients and set aside.
4. Combine .25 cup of the sweetener, coconut flour, walnuts, flaxseed meal, and sea salt in a mixing dish.
5. Add the butter and mix until it's crumbly. Set about .5 of a cup aside and add another teaspoon of sweetener.
6. Add the crumbled mixture to the pie plate and spread it out until flattened.
7. Pour in the fruit mixture over the crust. Sprinkle with the rest of the crust fixings.
8. Bake for 20 minutes with a layer of foil. Remove and cook the last 10 to 20 minutes until browned.
9. When done, place in the fridge to set.
10. Slice and enjoy when it's firm.

White Chocolate Bark

Yields Provided: 12 servings
Nutritional Macros - One Individual Serving:
- 0 g Net Carbs
- 0 g Total Protein
- 2 g Total Fats
- 40 Calories

Ingredient List:
- Cocoa butter (.25 cup)
- Low-carb sweetener (.33 cup)
- Vanilla powder (1 tsp.)
- Hemp seed powder (.5 tsp.)
- Toasted pumpkin seeds (1 tsp.)
- Salt (as desired)
- Coconut oil - for the bowl

Preparation Steps:
1. Chop the cocoa butter into fine bits. Add water to a double boiler and add the pieces to melt using the medium heat setting. Stir in the rest of the fixings.
2. Lightly grease a bowl using a spritz of oil and add the mixture.
3. Let it cool and break into 12 portions.

Cookies

Chocolate-Filled Peanut Butter Cookies

Yields Provided: 20 servings

Nutritional Macros - One Individual Serving:
- 2.7 g Net Carbs
- 4.5 g Total Protein
- 14 g Total Fats
- 150 Calories

Ingredient List:
- Almond flour (2.5 cups)
- Peanut butter (.5 cup)
- Coconut oil (.25 cup)
- Erythritol (.25 cup)
- Maple syrup (3 tbsp.)
- Vanilla extract (1 tbsp.)
- Baking powder (1.5 tsp.)
- Salt (.5 tsp.)
- Dark chocolate bars (2-3)

Preparation Steps:
1. Prepare the cookie pan with the paper.
2. Warm up the oven to reach 350° Fahrenheit.
3. Whisk each of the wet fixings together and mix in with the dry ingredients.
4. Mix well and place in the fridge for 20 to 30 minutes.
5. Break the bars into small squares. Shape the dough into little balls until they are flat.
6. Add one to two pieces of chocolate and seal into the ball.
7. Arrange on the cookie sheet.
8. Bake for about 15 minutes. Remove and serve.

Chocolate Fudge Haystacks

Yields Provided: 12 servings

Nutritional Macros - One Individual Serving:

- 1.5 g Net Carbs
- 2 g Total Protein
- 18 g Total Fats
- 172 Calories

Ingredient List:

- Softened cream cheese (4 oz.)
- Erythritol sweetener (.75 cup)
- Softened unsalted butter (.5 cup)
- Unsweetened cocoa powder (.25 cup)
- Coarse sea salt (.125 tsp.)
- Unsweetened desiccated/shredded coconut (1 cup)
- Sugar-free vanilla extract (1 tsp.)
- Chopped walnuts (.33 cups)

Preparation Steps:

1. Blend the cocoa powder, sweetener, cheese, and butter.
2. Stir in the walnuts, coconut, salt, and vanilla extract.
3. Scoop out one-inch balls to make haystacks. Chill for approximately 30 minutes or longer.
4. Store in the fridge or freezer for best results.

Chocolate Sea Salt Cookies

Yields Provided: 15 servings
Nutritional Macros - One Individual Serving:
- 1.6 g Net Carbs
- 3.4 g Total Protein
- 18.2 g Total Fats
- 188 Calories

Ingredient List:
- Unchilled coconut oil (.75 cup)
- Eggs (2)
- Vanilla extract (1 tsp.)
- Golden monk fruit sweetener (.75 cup)
- Unsweetened cocoa powder (2 tbsp.)
- Salt (.5 tsp.)
- Cream of tartar (.25 tsp.)
- Baking soda (.5 tsp.)
- Almond flour (2 cups)
- Flaky sea salt (as desired)

Preparation Steps:
1. Warm the oven in advance to baking to reach 350° Fahrenheit.
2. Set up two baking sheets with a layer of parchment baking paper.
3. Prepare using a hand mixer. Combine the eggs, coconut oil, and vanilla extract.
4. Toss in the sweetener, baking soda, cocoa powder, salt, and cream of tartar. Mix thoroughly.
5. Gradually fold in the almond flour.
6. Form the dough into balls. Place onto the baking sheet. Arrange them about two to three inches apart.
7. Garnish using the sea salt atop of each cookie.
8. Bake cookies for about 16 to 20 minutes; baking one tray at a time.
9. Remove and cool completely.
10. Gently pull the paper away from each of the cookies. Serve.

Coconut Chocolate Cookies

Yields Provided: 20 servings
Nutritional Macros - One Individual Serving:
- 1 g Net Carbs
- 2.2 g Total Protein
- 6.8 g Total Fats
- 77 Calories

Ingredient List:
- Almond flour (1 cup)
- Unsweetened shredded coconut (.33 cup)
- Erythritol (.33 cup)
- Baking powder (.5 tsp.)
- Cocoa powder (.25 cup)
- Coconut oil (.25 cup)
- Coconut flour (3 tbsp.)
- Salt (.25 tsp.)
- Vanilla extract (.25 tsp.)
- Unchilled eggs (2)

Preparation Steps:
1. Warm up the oven to 350° Fahrenheit. Cover a baking tin with a sheet of parchment baking paper.
2. Mix the dry fixings using a hand mixer.
3. In another mixing container, combine the wet ingredients and add to the dry until well blended.
4. Break apart pieces of the cookie dough and roll into 20 balls.
5. Arrange on the cookie sheet and bake for 15-20 minutes.

Italian Almond Macaroons

Yields Provided: 45 servings
Nutritional Macros - One Individual Serving:
- 0 g Net Carbs
- 2 g Total Protein
- 3 g Total Fats
- 31 Calories

Ingredient List:
- Almond flour about (2 cups plus 2 tbsp.)
- Monk fruit low-carb sweetener (.25 cup)
- Egg (2 whites)
- Almond extract (.5 tsp.)
- Powdered monk fruit sweetener - confectioners (1 tbsp.)

Preparation Steps:
1. Prepare a cookie sheet with a layer of parchment baking paper.
2. Combine the almond flour with the egg whites, sweetener, and almond extract. Knead the mixture until the dough is formed.
3. Form the dough into one-inch balls and place on the pan at least 1 inch apart. Bake at 250° Fahrenheit on the bottom rack of the oven for 55 to 60 minutes.
4. Remove the cookies from the baking pan to wire rack and dust using the confectioner's sweetener while still warm.

Pecan Turtle Truffles

Yields Provided: 15 servings
Nutritional Macros - One Individual Serving:
- 1 g Net Carbs
- 4 g Total Protein
- 14 g Total Fats
- 142 Calories

Ingredient List:
- Swerve or your preference (.33 cup)
- Melted butter (.5 cup)
- Vanilla extract (.25 tsp.)
- Caramel extract (.5 tsp.)
- Vanilla protein powder -0- carbs (.33 cup)
- Finely ground pecans (1 cup)
- 85% chocolate - Lindt or your choice (4 squares)
- Pecan halves (15)

Preparation Steps:
1. Combine the sweetener, butter, vanilla extract, caramel extracts, finely ground pecans, and protein powder in a mixing container.
2. Roll into 15 truffles and place on a sheet of parchment or waxed paper.
3. Melt the chocolate in a baggie in the microwave for one minute. Snip the corner and squeeze the chocolate over the prepared truffles.
4. Garnish each truffle with a pecan half. Chill and enjoy any time.

Pumpkin Cheesecake Cookies

Yields Provided: 15 servings
Nutritional Macros - One Individual Serving:
- 2 g Net Carbs
- 5 g Total Protein
- 15 g Total Fats
- 159 Calories

Ingredient List - Cookie Dough:
- Softened butter (6 tbsp.)
- Almond flour (2 cups)
- Solid-packed pumpkin puree (.33 cup)
- Large egg (1)
- Granulated erythritol sweetener (.75 cup)
- Baking powder (.5 tsp.)
- Nutmeg (.25 tsp.)
- Cinnamon (1 tsp.)
- Ground allspice (.125 tsp.)
- Salt (1 pinch)

Ingredient List - The Filling:
- Cream cheese (4 oz.)
- Vanilla (.5 tsp.)
- Large egg (1)
- Granulated erythritol sweetener (2 tbsp.)

Preparation Steps:
1. Heat the oven to 350° Fahrenheit.
2. Combine all of cookie dough ingredients in a medium-sized bowl and mix well until a dough forms. Scoop or spoon the cookie batter by about 1.5 tablespoons onto a parchment-lined baking sheet.
3. Use the back of the scoop or a round tablespoon measuring spoon to dent the tops of each cookie as shown in the photo collage in the post.
4. Combine the cream cheese, sweetener, egg, and vanilla in a magic bullet or small blender cup. Blend until smooth.
5. Pour the cream cheese filling into the tops of each cookie dent.
6. Bake the cookies until golden brown and the tops no longer jiggle (20 min.).
7. Remove and cool at least 10 minutes before eating.

Strawberry Thumbprint Delights

Yields Provided: 16 servings
Nutritional Macros - One Individual Serving:
- 1 g Net Carbs
- 2 g Total Protein
- 9 g Total Fats
- 95 Calories

Ingredient List:
- Almond flour (1 cup)
- Baking powder (.5 tsp.)
- Coconut flour (2 tbsp.)
- Sugar-free strawberry jam (2 tbsp.)
- Shredded coconut (1 tbsp.)
- Eggs (2)
- Erythritol (.5 cup)
- Coconut oil (4 tbsp.)
- Salt (.5 tsp.)
- Cinnamon (.5 tsp.)
- Almond extract (.5 tsp.)
- Vanilla extract (.5 tsp.)

Preparation Steps:
1. Warm up the oven temperature to 350° Fahrenheit.
2. Cover a cookie tin with a sheet of parchment paper.
3. Whisk the dry fixings and make a hole in the middle. Fold in the wet fixings to form a dough.
4. Break it into 16 segments and roll into balls.
5. Arrange each one on the prepared cookie sheet and bake 15 minutes.
6. When done, cool completely and add a dab of jam to each one with a sprinkle of coconut.

Streusel Scones

Yields Provided: 12 servings
Nutritional Macros - One Individual Serving:
- 3.5 g Net Carbs
- 0.6 g Total Protein
- 12 g Total Fats
- 145 Calories

Ingredient List:
- Baking powder (1 tsp.)
- Almond flour (2 cups)
- Ground stevia leaf (.25 tsp.)
- Fresh blueberries (1 cup)
- Egg (1)
- Salt (1 pinch)
- Almond milk (2 tbsp.)

Ingredient List - The Topping:
- Egg white (1 tbsp.)
- Ground cinnamon (.5 tsp.)
- Slivered almonds (.25 cup.)
- Stevia (1 pinch)

Preparation Steps:
1. Prepare the topping and set it aside.
2. Warm up the oven to 375° Fahrenheit.
3. Sift the baking powder, salt, flour, and stevia. Blend in the blueberries.
4. In another container, whisk the egg and milk until combined. Fold into the dry fixings and shape into 12 scones.
5. Arrange each of the scones on a parchment paper-lined baking tin.
6. Bake until golden brown or 20 to 22 minutes.
7. Add the prepared toppings serve.

Walnut Cookies

Yields Provided: 16 servings
Nutritional Macros - One Individual Serving:
- 1.1 g Net Carbs
- 3 g Total Protein
- 6.7 g Total Fats
- 72 Calories

Ingredient List:
- Egg (1)
- Ground cinnamon (1 tsp.)
- Erythritol (2 tbsp.)
- Ground walnuts (1.5 cups)

Preparation Steps:
1. Warm up the oven to reach 350° Fahrenheit. Prepare a baking tin with a sheet of parchment baking paper.
2. Combine the cinnamon and erythritol with the egg. Fold in the walnuts.
3. Shape into balls and bake for 10 to 13 minutes. Cool slightly and serve.

Conclusion

I hope you have enjoyed each segment of your new *Ketogenic Sweet Treats Cookbook*. I hope it was informative and provided you with all of the tools you need to achieve your goals whatever they may be. Enjoy every sweet moment by following the items outlined! The next step is to decide which tempting treat you should choose first. Just sit down and make a shopping list of all of the items you want to prepare.

Stay determined and stand by your goals during your transition to ketosis. Follow the instructions and recipe methods. Before long, you will be able to quickly scan recipes and know before you finish reading how healthy they are for you and your family. The most significant benefit is that you are never hungry using the keto diet plan.

You will need to formulate a game plan as you begin your ketogenic diet plan. That will include keeping track of your macronutrients. You can use any form you choose whether it is keeping a written journal or using an app. These are a few tips to get you started:

Use A Standard Keto Calculator: You will achieve the perfect mixture of the traditional keto diet plan of 5% carbs, 25% protein, and 70% ratios. (This is a general ratio.) Begin your weight loss process by making a habit of checking your levels when you want to know what essentials your body needs during the course of your dieting plan. You will document your personal information such as height and weight. The Internet calculator will provide you with essential math.

Check Units of Measurement: Many of the recipes you will discover over the Internet or other sources may be listed in Imperial (ex. pounds) or in the Metric system.

You will learn how to make all of the decisions needed to be successful with your new way of living. You will know when you have the time to prepare it and how it will fit in with your macro counts.

However, you cannot live on desserts alone. Do you know how to handle the cravings you will experience on the keto plan? These are a few to help keep your ketosis in line outside of the dessert table:

Chocolate: The carbon, magnesium, and chromium levels are requesting a portion of spinach, nuts, and seeds, or some broccoli and cheese. However, if you're craving chocolate, eat chocolate. You need to make sure you eat 75% or higher dark chocolate - not milk chocolate.

Sugary Foods: Several things can trigger the desire for sugar, but typically phosphorous, and tryptophan are the culprits. Have some chicken, beef, lamb, liver, cheese, cauliflower, or broccoli.

Salty Foods: If your body is craving foods such as pizza and chips, your body may be craving silicon. Have a few nuts and seeds; just be sure to count them into your daily counts. You may also be craving chloride or tryptophan. Munch on unsalted cottage cheese, cheese, fish, or spinach and add salt.

Why not get started right now? There is no need to wait. You will have the plan, the recipes, and now the knowledge to use your chosen fasting option with the delicious ketogenic lifestyle you have chosen to lead. Enjoy a cup of delicious Bulletproof Coffee! This recipe has you calculated for one cup:

Nutritional Macros - One Individual Serving:
- 0 g Net Carbs
- 1 g Total Protein
- 51 g Total Fats
- 463 Calories

Ingredient List:
- MCT oil powder (2 tbsp.)
- Ghee or butter (2 tbsp.)
- Hot coffee (1.5 cups)

Preparation Steps:
1. Prepare and pour the hot coffee into your blender.
2. Add in the powder and ghee/butter. Blend until frothy.
3. Serve in a large mug.

Finally, if you found this book useful in any way, a review on Amazon is always appreciated!

Index For The Recipes

Chapter 2: Muffins & Bagels

1. Almond & Apple Maple Muffins
2. Banana Avocado Muffins
3. Blueberry Flaxseed Muffins
4. Cinnamon Walnut Flax Muffins
5. Coconut Lemon Muffins
6. Peanut Butter Muffins - Instant Pot
7. Pecan Pie & Chocolate Muffins
8. Pumpkin & Maple Flaxseed Muffins

Bagels

1. Cinnamon Raisin Bagels

Chapter 3: Cakes
Regular Cakes

1. Carrot & Almond Cake
2. Chocolate & Zucchini Cake
3. Chocolate Lava Cake
4. Glazed Pound Cake
5. Gooey Butter Cake
6. Orange Rum Cake
7. Pumpkin Bread
8. Slow-Cooked Raspberry Coconut Cake

Bar Cakes

1. Almond Coconut Bars
2. Cheesecake Mocha Bars
3. Chocolate Peppermint Cookie Bars
4. Coconut Bars
5. Keto Magic Bars
6. Mixed Berry Cake Bars
7. Peanut Butter Protein Bars

Cupcakes & Mug Cakes

1. Blueberry Cupcakes
2. Brownie Mug Cake - Instant Pot
3. Chocolate Mug Cake
4. Pumpkin Spice Cupcakes
5. Sour Cream Vanilla Cupcakes
6. Vanilla Berry Mug Cake
7. Zucchini Spiced Cupcakes

Chapter 4: Fat Bombs & Pies

1. Blackberry Coconut Fat Bombs
2. Blueberry Fat Bombs
3. Cheesecake Surprise Fat Bombs
4. Chocolate Chip Cookie Dough Fat Bomb
5. Cocoa Butter Walnut Fat Bombs
6. Coconut Macaroon Fat Bombs
7. Coconut Orange Creamsicle Fat Bombs
8. Coffee Fat Bombs
9. Dark Chocolate Fat Bombs
10. Lemon Cheesecake Fat Bombs
11. Neapolitan Fat Bombs
12. Orange & Walnut Chocolate Fat Bombs
13. Peppermint & Chocolate Fat Bombs
14. Stuffed Pecan Fat Bombs

Pies

1. Creamy Lime Pie
2. Pumpkin Cheesecake Pie
3. Sour Cream Lemon Pie
4. Low-Carb Almond Flour Crust
5. Mini Coconut Pies

Chapter 5: Delicious Mousse & Pudding Options

1. Cheesecake Pudding
2. Chocolate & Avocado Pudding
3. Cinnamon Roll Mousse In A Jar
4. Peanut Butter Mousse
5. Pumpkin Custard
6. Raspberry Chia Pudding
7. White Chocolate Mousse

Chapter 6: Frozen Desserts

1. Butter Pecan Ice Cream
2. Coconut Ice Cream

3. Egg-Fast Vanilla Frozen Custard
4. Peanut Butter Ice Cream
5. Pistachio Ice Cream
6. Thick Dark Chocolate Milkshake

Smoothies

1. Almond & Blueberry Smoothie
2. Avocado Smoothie
3. Avocado Mint Green Smoothie
4. Banana Bread - Blueberry Smoothie
5. Blackberry Cheesecake Smoothie
6. Blueberry Yogurt Smoothie
7. Chocolate & Cinnamon Smoothie
8. Cinnamon Roll Smoothie
9. Cucumber Spinach Smoothies
10. Delightful Chocolate Smoothie
11. Mexican Chocolate Smoothie
12. Mint Chocolate Smoothie
13. Mocha Smoothie
14. Pecan Pie Smoothie
15. Smoothie In A Bowl
16. Strawberry & Rhubarb Pie Smoothie
17. Strawberry Smoothies
18. Vanilla Fat-Burning Smoothie

Chapter 7: Snacks

1. Apple Cider Donut Bites
2. Baked Almonds & Brie
3. Baked Apples
4. Blueberry Tart
5. Chocolate Coconut Bites
6. Cinnamon Vanilla Protein Bites
7. Cream Cheese Truffles
8. Peanut Butter & Coconut Balls
9. Pumpkin Blondies
10. Strawberries With Coconut Whip
11. Strawberry & Cream Cakes
12. Strawberry Rhubarb Crumble
13. White Chocolate Bark

Cookies

1. Chocolate-Filled Peanut Butter Cookies
2. Chocolate Fudge Haystacks
3. Chocolate Sea Salt Cookies
4. Coconut Chocolate Cookies

5. Italian Almond Macaroons
6. Pecan Turtle Truffles
7. Pumpkin Cheesecake Cookies
8. Strawberry Thumbprint Delights
9. Streusel Scones
10. Walnut Cookies

Description

Would you like to own a book that includes a ton of delicious desserts that are allowed on your keto diet plan?

Are you on the ketogenic way of life and enjoy desserts but need more to add to your special collection?

Have you reached your limit for seeking new keto recipes to only find they are not keto-friendly?

Set aside all of those questions and enjoy your keto experience using the Keto Sweet Treats Cookbook. Start by improving your table rules using these tips:

Remember to skip the highest ranks of GPS – grains, potatoes, and sugar.

Use a smaller plate. Play a mind game and fill a small plate instead of a larger one. Try it, this really works.

Take your time. Enjoy your time spend with the conversation of a friend or family member. Drink your water and sip your tea or coffee. Enjoy and feel satisfied!

Focus on veggies, fats, and proteins. Visit a restaurant that offers a healthy salad bar, seafood spreads, carving stations, and vegetable platters. You can usually find butter, olive oil, sour cream, and cheese in plentiful supply.

Make Wise Drink Decisions: The best choice is water, tea, coffee, or sparkling water. Decaf coffee or herbal tea is another excellent option. If alcohol is your craving, choose dry wine, champagne, or light beer. Also, consider spirits – straight or with a bit of club soda.

Choose Dessert Wisely: If you are still hungry, try to have another cup of tea or a cheese platter. Have a portion of berries with heavy cream. What about some cream in your coffee?

You can enjoy your favorite desserts anytime. Just see what these two performers have to say:

- *Lebron James:* This baller slimmed down and showed off his 6-pack in 2014 which he later revealed that the keto diet was the major influence of his success story. He didn't consume carbohydrates, sugar, or dairy products. It works!

- *Halle Berry:* Halle Berry turned 50 years old and credited the ketogenic diet for keeping her fit. She also stated that it works well with her diabetes.

- *Mick Jagger:* The Rolling Stones frontman gets "Satisfaction" from the ketogenic diet that has added years to his life.

- *Kim Kardashian:* Kim dropped over 50 pounds of baby weight on a Y low carb, ketogenic style diet by consuming less than 60 grams of carbs per day.

No matter how busy you are, preparing a healthy and balanced meal should be your first priority. If you wish to succeed in your health and fitness goals, you can begin by enjoying healthier choices in the dessert line by better understanding how they are properly prepared.

If that isn't enough to tempt you; try one of these delicious treats when you purchase your new cookbook:

- Streusel Scones
- Cheesecake Pudding
- Peppermint & Chocolate Fat Bombs
- Creamy Lime Pie
- Pecan Pie Smoothie

Start by adding this *Ketogenic Sweet Treats Cookbook* to your personal library today! Be watchful for upcoming books with tons of new recipes!

Have a new sweet treat every day!

Made in the USA
Monee, IL
21 May 2020